THE CHARM OF
THE ENGLISH
VILLAGE

Preston on Stour, Gloucestershire.

THE CHARM OF THE ENGLISH VILLAGE

P. H. DITCHFIELD

ILLUSTRATED BY SYDNEY R. JONES

SENATE

The Charm of the English Village

This edition published in 1994 by Senate, an imprint of Studio Editions Ltd, Princess House, 50 Eastcastle Street, London W1N 7AP, England

ISBN 1 85958 030 0
Printed and bound in Guernsey by The Guernsey Press Co Ltd

CONTENTS

THE CHARM
OF THE ENGLISH VILLAGE

I

THE VILLAGE

NO country in the world can boast of possessing rural homes and villages which have half the charm and picturesqueness of our English cottages and hamlets.   Wander where you will, in Italy or Switzerland, France or Germany, and when you return home you will be bound to confess that in no foreign land have you seen a village which for beauty and interest can compare with the scattered hamlets of our English land. These others may be surrounded by grander scenery and finer landscapes.   The monotonous blue sea of the Mediterranean may lave their feet ; lofty, snow-clad mountains may tower above chalets and homesteads ; the romance of the Rhine, the vine-clad slopes, may produce a certain amount of attractiveness ; but when you return to England and contrast our peaceful homely villages with all that you have seen, you will have learned to appreciate their real charm.   They have to be known in order that they may be loved.   They do not force themselves upon our notice.   The hasty visitor may pass them by, and miss half their attractiveness.   They have to be wooed in varying moods in order that they may display their charms, when the blossoms are bright in the village orchards, when the sun shines on the streams and pools and gleams upon the glories of old thatch, when autumn has tinged the trees with golden tints, or when the hoar-frost makes their bare branches beautiful again with new and glistening foliage. Not even in their summer garb do they look more beautiful.

One of the causes of the charm of an English village arises from the sense of their stability. Nothing changes in our country life. The old tower of the village church that has looked down upon generation after generation of the inhabitants seems to say, "*Je suis, je reste*. All things change but I. I see the infant brought here to be christened. A few years pass ; the babe has grown to be an old man and is borne here, and sleeps under my shadow. Age after age passes, but I survive." One of the most graceful of English writers tells tenderly of this sense of the stability of our village life :—"On the morning of Charles I's execution,—in the winters and springs when Elizabeth was Queen,—when Becket lay dead on Canterbury steps,—when Harold was on his way to Senlac,—that hill, that path were there—sheep were climbing it, and shepherds were herding them. It has been so since England began—it will be so when I am dead. We are only shadows that pass. But England lives always—and shall live." [1]

Another charm of our villages is their variety. There are no two villages exactly the same. Each one possesses its own individuality, its own history, peculiarities, and architectural distinction. Church, manor-house, farm and cottage, differ somewhat in each village. You never see two churches or two houses exactly alike, just as the Great Architect scarcely ever has framed two faces exactly similar. It is true that the style is traditional, that each son learned from his sire how to build, and followed the plans and methods of his forefathers ; but he never slavishly imitated their work.

[1] Mrs. Humphry Ward, *The Testing of Diana Mallory.*

WEOBLEY, HEREFORDSHIRE

He introduced improvements devised by his own ingenuity and skill, created picturesque effects which added beauty to the building. Sometimes his purse was full with the price of his rich fleeces, and he could afford to adorn his home with more elaborate decoration ; sometimes *res angusta domi*, when times were bad, compelled him to aim at greater simplicity with no less satisfactory results.

Another cause of variety in the appearance of our village buildings is the different nature of the materials used in their construction. Geology plays no small part in the production of various styles of village architecture. In the days of our forefathers, in Elizabethan or Jacobean times, there were no railroads to transport slates from Wales, or dump down wagon-loads of bricks or beams of timber in a country that possessed good stone-quarries. They were obliged to use the materials which nature in their own district afforded. This was the great secret of their success. Nature's productions harmonise best with the face of nature in the district where they are produced. Alien buildings have always an unsatisfactory appearance ; and if we modern folk would build with good effect, we must use the natural material provided by the quarries, or woods, or clay-pits indigenous to the district, and not transport our materials from afar.

There is an immense variety in the building stone of England. There are the sandstones ; the Old Red Sandstone of Cheshire, Shropshire, and Herefordshire, which cannot long resist the weather, but is a beautiful material and harmonises well with the surrounding scenery ; the New Sandstone of Tunbridge Wells and many places in Yorkshire, and is extremely durable ; the Reigate variety, the best of the *firestones* which the old builders used for the stately castle of Windsor, Hampton Court, and other palatial buildings round London. Then there are the limestone quarries, which yield the best of material for building. You see splendid edifices all along the course

4

FARLEIGH HUNGERFORD, SOMERSET

of this formation extending from Somerset through the Midlands to the dales of Yorkshire. Chilmark supplied the grand stone for Salisbury Cathedral and Wilton Abbey ; Tottenhoe in the Midlands gave us Dunstable Church and Woburn Abbey and Luton ; Belvoir and Chatsworth derived their stone from Worksworth, Derbyshire ; Ancaster in Lincolnshire has yielded material for many good buildings ;

BERRYNARBOR, DEVON

and Tadcaster has built York Minster, Beverley, and Ripon. Kentish rag found near Maidstone is as hard as iron, but is good for rough walling. Then there is the great division of oolitic limestone, of which the Barnack, Bath, and Portland oolites are the best. All these quarries have yielded material for great buildings as well as for the humbler village churches, cottages, and manor-houses which it is our pleasure to visit.

Where stone is scarce and forests plentiful our builders

PORLOCK WEIR, SOMERSET

made use of timber, especially in the south-eastern district, where half-timbered houses form a wondrous charm to all who admire their beauties. Now we get our timber from Russia, Norway, Sweden, and America ; but our ancestors loved nothing more than good old English oak, and oak abounded in many parts of the country, in the south-eastern counties, Herefordshire, Shropshire, Cheshire, and Lancashire, where some grand timber houses may be found. Brick and flint are the principal substances of East Anglia building and in many other parts of England ; and houses built of the dark, dull, thin old bricks, not of the great staring modern varieties, are very charming, especially when they are seen against a background of wooded hills.

Cornish cottages are built of granite and cling to the valley sides, so that one can hardly distinguish between the living rock and the built wall. The moor-side dwellings on the rugged hills of Cumberland and Westmoreland are also constructed of granite and roofed with slate, and look lonely and desolate in their bleak surroundings.

There is, therefore, an endless variety in the style, architecture, and appearance of our villages which is one of their chief charms. Our artist transports us to various parts of England, and his drawings show the immense variety in the appearances of our villages. He has travelled through many counties, sketching with skilful pen each beautiful view, each characteristic building. We journey with him to the West and note the fine " black and white " houses in Weobley village, Herefordshire (p. 3), the picturesque village of Farleigh Hungerford (p. 5), six miles from Bath, and some old cottages at Berrynarbor, Devon. Fishing villages on the sea-coast have a style of their own with their little harbours, wooden piers, and their fishing boats. An example of one of these quaint old ports is shown in the sketch of Porlock Weir, Somerset. Northwards we fly to picturesque Derbyshire, where high towering peaks and lovely scenery

STANTON·IN·THE·PEAK, DERBYSHIRE

add again another element of variety to the appearance of the villages that nestle among the hills, and where good building stone affords a fine material for the erection of village dwelling-places. We see the little village of Stoney Middleton encircled by rocks and hills, and Stanton-in-the Peak, a pretty glimpse of a village street. Northampton-

STONEY MIDDLETON, DERBYSHIRE

shire, too, has some grand stone for building purposes. No county is richer than this one for its noble churches. A typical Northamptonshire village is Moreton Pinkney, of which a sketch is shown.

The three counties which compose the Oxford diocese, Berks, Bucks, and Oxfordshire, have many pretty villages.

MORETON PINKNEY, NORTHANTS

SUTTON COURTNEY, BERKS

Sutton Courtney, Berks, reminds us of the monks of Abingdon who had a grange there, and of the noble family of the Courtneys who held one of the manors and possessed a manor-house, which retains a Norman doorway and the chapel. West Wycombe, Bucks, is a picturesque village (p. 14)

WATLINGTON, OXON

stretching along the main road towards Stokenchurch, famous for its extraordinary church built in 1763 by Lord le Despencer, Francis Dashwood, one of the Medmenham "monks" of evil fame. The building shown on the right of the sketch has a projecting clock and is known as the church-loft. Beneath it are labourers' cottages. Watlington is a small market-town, scarcely larger than a village. The sketch shows the old market-house built in 1664 by Thomas Stonor, standing at the meeting of four cross-roads. It is not unlike that of Ross on the Wye, and, with its mullioned windows, high pointed gables, and dark arches, is a favourite subject for artists.

A good example of a Suffolk village is shown in the sketch of Cavendish (p. 17), with its church and cottages

WEST WYCOMBE, BUCKS

clustering round it like children holding the gown of their good mother, and in the foreground the village green, the scene of many a rural revel. Biddenden, Kent, reminds us of the famous maids who left a bequest for the distributing of doles of bread and cheese on Easter Sunday, and of the remarkable cakes, each stamped with a representation of the foundresses of the feast, who are supposed to have been linked together like the Siamese Twins. This quiet and

BIDDENDEN, KENT

SELBORNE, HANTS, FROM THE HANGER

remote village possesses some charming half-timbered cottages, as the sketch shows.

A pleasing sketch of historic Selborne, Hants, the village immortalised by Gilbert White, is shown, and the beauties of Ringwood stand revealed when viewed in the subdued light of a stormy sunset. The Isle of Wight abounds with fine specimens of picturesque villages and prettily situated cottages. A view of Carisbrook taken from the castle hill

CAVENDISH, SUFFOLK

is shown (p. 21), and of Godshill village (p. 19), with its thatched cottages and good church tower.

In spite of the endless variety of our villages it is not difficult to note their main characteristics, and to try to describe a typical example. We see arising above the trees the village church, the centre of the old village life, both religious, secular, and social. The building has been altered and added to at various times, and now shows, writ in stone, its strange and varied history. The work of Norman masons and of the builders of subsequent periods can be

A STORMY SUNSET, RINGWOOD, HANTS

GODSHILL VILLAGE, ISLE OF WIGHT

seen in its walls and sculptures, and also the hand of "restorers" who have dealt hardly with its beauties, and in trying to renovate have often destroyed its chief attractions. We will examine it more particularly in a subsequent chapter.

Nestling amid the trees we see the manor-house, the abode of the squire, an ancient dwelling-place of Tudor or Jacobean design, surrounded by a moat, with a good terrace-walk in front, and a formal garden with fountain and sun-dial and beds in arabesque. It seems to look down upon the village with a sort of protecting air. Near at hand are some old farm-houses, nobly built, with no vain pretension about them. Carefully thatched ricks and barns and stables and cow-sheds stand around them.

There is a village inn with its curiously painted sign-board which has a story to tell of the old coaching days, and of the great people who used to travel along the main roads and were sometimes snowed up in a drift just below "the Magpie," but could always find good accommodation in the inn, beds with lavender-scented sheets, plain, well-cooked English joints, and every attention. Perhaps the village can boast of an ancient castle or a monastery, the ruins of which add beauty and picturesqueness to its appearance.

An old almshouse, a peaceful retreat for the aged and infirm, built by some pious benefactor in ages long gone by, attracts our gaze, a beautiful Jacobean structure, perhaps, with the chapel in one wing and the master's house in the other. Nor did the good people of former days forget the advantages of education. There is an old school which modern Government inspectors can scarcely be persuaded to allow to live, because it is not framed according to modern plans and ideas. Some villages can boast of a grammar school, too—Secondary Schools they call them now—the buildings of which are not the least attractive features of the place.

The village green still remains to remind us of the gaiety

CARISBROOK FROM THE CASTLE HILL, ISLE OF WIGHT

of old village life, where the old country dances were in-
dulged in by the villagers, and the merry May-pole reared.
There they held their rural sports, and fought bouts of
quarter-staff and cudgel-play, and played pipe and tabor at
many a rustic feast.

No country in the world has so many beautiful examples
of cottage architecture as England. We will examine, with
the aid of our artist, many of these old buildings with the
thatched roofs and general comeliness. The old village
crosses, too, will arrest our attention, and much else that
interests us, as we walk through the streets and lanes of an
English village. With our artist's aid we will examine each
feature of the village more particularly. We need not concern ourselves now with the buried treasure of old village
history, though these constitute some of its chiefest attractions. It will be enough for us to use our eyes and note
each beauty and perfection, and thus try to learn something
of the charm of an English village.

II

THE VILLAGE CHURCH

IN the centre of the village stands the church, always
the most important and interesting building in the
place. It appears in several of our illustrations of
typical English villages. In the view of King's
Norton, with the village green in the foreground and the
half-timbered houses, the lofty spire of the church rises
high above the trees and whispers a *sursum corda*. Ditcheat
Church (p. 27) stands in a region famous for its noble ecclesi-
astical edifices and fine towers. It is mainly fifteenth-century
work. We will inspect an ordinary village church which has
not been too much "restored" or renovated, and observe its
numerous interesting features.

First, at the entrance of "God's acre" stands the lych-
gate, the gate of the dead, usually protected by a broad
overspreading gable roof in order that those who accom-
pany the bodies of the faithful to their last resting-place may
meet before going to the church, and may be protected from
the weather. The gate at Clun, Shropshire (p. 26), is shown
in our illustrations, a graceful four-gabled structure with
tiled roof. The well-known gate at Bray, Berkshire, has a
room over it. Entering the churchyard we recall Gray's
poem, and note the place wherein

> The rude forefathers of the hamlet sleep,

too often left uncared for, like that shown in the sketch
at Shere (p. 29). The quaint inscriptions on the gravestones,

the curious productions of a rustic muse, excite interest, and the sombreness of the scene is relieved by many a touch of strange humour, such as the lines in memory of a parish clerk in Shenley churchyard, who was also a bricklayer :

> Silent in dust lies mouldering here
> A Parish clerk of voice most clear.
> None Joseph Rogers could excel
> In laying bricks or singing well;
> Though snapp'd his line, laid by his rod,
> We build for him our hopes in God.

The church itself is an ancient structure. It consists of a nave and chancel, and perhaps one or two aisles have been added to the nave, or a chantry chapel built on the north or south side of the chancel containing the tombs and monuments of some illustrious family connected with the place. Many Norman churches are cruciform, with a low tower rising at the intersection of the nave with the transepts. Frequently the tower stands at the west end. Various kinds of towers exist. We have the low Norman tower, frequently raised in subsequent periods and surmounted with a spire, the weight of which has sorely tried the early Norman building, and has often caused it to collapse; round towers, towers highly enriched with turrets and parapets and crowned with a lofty spire. The external buttresses which support the walls indicate very clearly the period of the building. Norman buttresses extend very little from the walls, which were so strong that they needed little external support. As the builders strove after lightness and increased the size of the windows, larger and more extended buttresses were needed, until we get to flying buttresses, i.e. those of an outer wall connected by an arch to those of an inner, producing very graceful and beautiful effects. Niches for statues are often carved on the buttresses. Curious grotesquely carved heads and figures look down upon us from the gutters of the roofs—called gargoyles. The style and

KING'S NORTON FROM THE GREEN, WORCESTERSHIRE

period of the windows are no indication of the age of the walls in which they appear. Very frequently windows of a later style were inserted in place of others of an older age. Thus Norman walls frequently have Perpendicular windows. The porch is a large structure with a gable having bargeboards similar to those seen in old houses. It is built of

LYCH GATE, CLUN, SHROPSHIRE

wood and roofed with tiles. There are seats on either side the porch. Sometimes we have stone porches with a room above, called a parvise, which occasionally has a piscina, showing that there must have been an altar there. This chamber was used as a priest's room, or by the custodian of the church who guarded its treasures; in some cases as an anchor-hold, or room set apart for the use of an anchorite

DITCHEAT CHURCH, SOMERSET

or recluse. The doors of churches are an interesting study. Here in this typical village church we find a doorway embellished with curious Romanesque carving, the only remains of the old Norman church, except that the wall in which it is placed is probably of the same date, though it is pierced by a lancet and two Perpendicular windows. This doorway has a succession of receding semicircular arches enriched with a variety of sculptured mouldings, zigzag, cable, star, embattled, and beak-heads. These last are monsters with long beaks, meant to represent the devil and his angels ready to pounce upon the souls of those who come to church in a heedless and irreverent spirit. The door itself is the original one with large elaborate crescent-shaped hinges and a triple strap ornamented with scrolls and foliage, like that at Stillingfleet. These strong doors were intended to protect the church from marauders, from northern pirates, and such-like folk. Above the door is the tympanum on which is carved the *Agnus Dei*. A great variety of subjects appear on these tympana—Adam and Eve, St. George and the Dragon, the Tree of Life, signs of the Zodiac, and very many other symbolical representations. Above the doorway is a niche, now shorn of its image, but probably once containing the statue of our Lord or the Virgin. You will notice on the stones of the doorway rude crosses scratched with a knife which are votive crosses made hundreds of years ago by persons who had made some vow, or desired thus mutely to express their thankfulness for some special and private mercy.

On entering the church we see the font, an old Norman one, decorated with mouldings and sculpture. It is lined with lead, and on the sides are rudely carved the four evangelists with their symbols. The roof is much flatter than an earlier one which once spanned the church, as the marks on the tower show. This one was erected in the fifteenth century with tie-beams extending from wall to wall, and

"GOD'S ACRE," SHERE, SURREY

resting on uprights placed on corbels, and underneath the beams are curved bracing-ribs which meet in the centre of the beam and form an arch. Above the centre of the beam is a king-post, and the vacant space is occupied by pierced panels. This sloping portion of the roof is divided into squares by pieces of timber called purlins, which are adorned with mouldings and bosses at their intersections.

The nave is now filled with pews; most of them are quite new, but in one corner we find a few of the old seats richly

HOUR-GLASS BRACKET, SOUTH
STOKE CHURCH, OXON

carved with poppy-heads, which, I need not say, have nothing to do with the flower. Happily all the old-fashioned high square pews which once disfigured the church have been removed, and these modern seats are somewhat like the more primitive models.

There is a very fine Jacobean pulpit similar to that at Little Hadham Church, Hertfordshire, though not quite so elaborate. In 1603 churchwardens were ordered to provide in every church a " comely and decent pulpit," and although some few mediæval examples remain, most of our pulpits have

LITTLE HADHAM CHURCH, HERTFORDSHIRE

been erected since the first year of King James I. A necessary accessory to the pulpit in the days of long sermons was
the hour-glass, which a merciless preacher would sometimes
turn and "have another glass." Very few of the actual glasses
remain, but we have numerous examples of beautiful ironwork brackets which once supported the preacher's timepiece.
A fine specimen is shown in our illustrations. It is in the
church of South Stoke, Oxfordshire, and at Hurst and
Binfield in Berkshire we have some magnificent examples of
elaborate ironwork hour-glass stands.

The church of Little Hadham retains its screen. Very
many have been destroyed. Our typical church has a richly
carved example painted and gilded, and on the north of the
chancel arch is a staircase which once led to the rood-loft,
where was a crucifix with the images of the Virgin and St. John
on each side. The old stone altar marked with its five crosses
has disappeared. It was destroyed at the Reformation, but
there is a good modern altar with a fine old reredos richly
ornamented with niches which formerly held statues. These
have all disappeared. The east window contains some good
decorated glass. The piscina and sedilia with their fine carv-
ings all merit attention, and the aumbries now shorn of their
doors wherein the church plate was formerly kept. The
Easter sepulchre, the wooden stalls with their quaintly carved
misereres (this church of ours was once attached to a
monastic cell connected with the great abbey of A——), must
all be noticed, and the verger will tell you that these were
ingenious traps for sleepy monks, who when the heavy seat fell
down with a loud bang, were detected in slumber and were
forced to do penance ; but if you are wise, you will not
believe him. He will also tell you that a little low side
window was really a leper's window, through which the poor
afflicted one could view the elevation of the host ; and again,
if you are wise, you will not believe him, as you know the
lepers were not even allowed to enter the churchyard.

THE VILLAGE CHURCH

Some curious old mural paintings have recently been discovered beneath layers of whitewash, and we notice the figure of St. Nicholas raising to life the three youths thrown into a tub, and a huge St. Christopher, a very favourite subject, as a glance at him would secure the observer from violent death throughout the day, and protect him from wandering thoughts during the service.

Then there are the brasses to examine, the beautiful monuments of old knights and warriors, fine ladies with great ruffs praying at faldstools opposite their husbands with a crowd of children beneath them, and gigantic monuments of great ladies who possessed every imaginable virtue. Some of the knights have their legs crossed, and the vicar or the verger will tell you that they had fought in the crusades. That one whose feet are crossed at the ankles went to one crusade ; that other one whose feet are crossed at the knees fought twice in the Holy Land ; and the third knight with feet crossed at the thighs fought three times in the Holy Wars. Again you will not believe him, if you are wise, because you know that these interpretations of a curious fashion are fallacious, that some knights who fought in the crusades are not so represented, and that others who never left England have their feet crossed. It was a passing whim or fashion and has no particular signification.

The bells with their quaint inscriptions, if you have a mind to ascend the belfry tower, may interest you, and the church plate, and the contents of the Parish Chest, invite inspection. The chest itself, with its elaborate lock and iron-bound sides, is a great treasure. One of the chief charms of an English village is to ransack this chest and examine carefully the registers, the churchwardens' accounts, the briefs, and many an old document that Time has failed to destroy. But this would lead us into too wide a field, and we must content ourselves with but a hasty survey of the village church and all the varied beauties and interesting objects which it contains.

III

MANORS, FARMS, AND RECTORIES

A LMOST every village has its giants as well as its dwarfs, its tritons as well as its minnows. You see its grander and finer specimens of English domestic architecture as well as the humbler dwellings of the poor. We will endeavour to examine in this chapter the former, the manor-house, the rectory or vicarage, and the farm-houses, three styles of houses which have much in common, though they maintain their own characteristics.

Some villages possess a great and important mansion, wherein some noble family resides, a glorified manor-house, Elizabethan or Jacobean perhaps, more commonly a Palladian structure built in the Italian manner, which has supplanted an earlier house and not improved upon the old English model. There was at one time a fashion for pulling down old Tudor or Elizabethan houses and rearing these Italian mansions. Very grand they are and ornate, but not over comfortable to live in. A great wit advised the builder of one of these mansions to hire a room on the other side of the road, and spend his time looking at his Palladian house, but to be sure not to live there. But our typical village does not possess a mansion; no Longleat or Haddon, no Lacock or Hardwick add to its importance; nor is it fortunate enough to have a castle. Its charm would be mightily increased if it could boast of such a venerable building, though the castle were but a ruin, a memorial of ancient state and power. Our artist has depicted one such castle,

HURSTMONCEUX CASTLE, SUSSEX

that of Hurstmonceux, in Sussex, which was at one time the largest and finest of the commoners' houses in the county, and was built in the fifteenth century. It was built of hard Flemish brick, with windows, door-cases, and copings of stone. The brickwork, sometimes said to be the earliest in England,[1] has long worn a greyish tint. The sketch shows the entrance gateway flanked by two towers with machiolations and pierced with embrasures for bowmen. The two towers are crowned by turrets, named the watch and signal turrets. A moat surrounds the castle, and was spanned by a drawbridge, the vertical slits on each side of the central recessed window being fitted with levers for raising and lowering the bridge. Over the archway are the arms of the Fiennes family, a wolf-dog with its paws on a banner and three lions rampant. If we were to pass through this gate we should find the ruins of an immense castle, a veritable town. Grouped round the green court, which is girt by a cloister, we see the remains of the great hall, a noble room, the postern gate with chapel over it, prison, pantries, bird gallery, armour gallery, ale-cellar, a grand staircase, with drawing-room, great parlour, bedchambers sufficient to lodge a garrison, and ladies' bower; while from the Pump Court we see the laundry, brewhouse, bakehouse, and a vast kitchen, still-room, confectioner's room, and countless other apartments. The castle was indeed a noble and hospitable mansion in olden time. The castle was built in the days of transition, when the strong uncomfortable fortress was giving place to a more luxurious mansion, though the necessity of strong walls and gates had not quite passed away. We need not concern ourselves with its history. Its name preserves the memories of two ancient families, De Hurst and De Monceaux, and was built in 1440 by Sir Roger Fiennes, one of the heroes of Agincourt and treasurer

---

[1] Little Wenham Hall, Suffolk, built of brick in the time of Henry III, is older than Hurstmonceux, and also the chapel of Little Coggeshall, Essex.

THE HAUNTED HALL, HARVINGTON, WORCESTERSHIRE

of Henry VI. His descendants had the title of Lord Dacre conferred upon them, and the last became Earl of Sussex, marrying a natural daughter of Charles II, and being impecunious sold the property. Its subsequent history does not concern us. The ghosts of its great owners seem to haunt the scene of their former splendour, and one noted uneasy spirit inhabited Drummer's hall, and marched along the battlements beating a devil's tattoo on his drum. But perhaps he was only a gardener in league with the smugglers, and used this ghostly means for conveying to them a needful signal. Ghosts often frequent the old houses of England, and our artist's sketch of the haunted house, Harvington Hall, Worcestershire, which looks delightfully picturesque in the moonlight, certainly suggests the appearance of a ghostly resident or visitor. We know of such a house in Lancashire, which, like Harvington·Hall, is encircled by a moat. It contains a skull in a case let into the wall of the staircase. This skull has been cast into the moat, buried in the ground, and removed in many other ways ; but terrible happenings ensue : storms rage and lightnings flash, and groans are heard, until the skull is brought back to its niche, when peace ensues. Some say the skull is that of a Roman priest beheaded at Lancaster ; others that it once graced the body of Roger Downes, the last heir of the house, one of the wildest courtiers of Charles II. These ancient traditions, ghosts and legends, add greatly to the charm of our old houses.

Leaving the mansions of the great, we will visit the usual chief house of the village, the manor-house, where the lord of the manor lived and ruled in former days, administered justice, and was the friend and benefactor of every one in the village. In times gone by the squire was an important factor in the village commonwealth. His place was at home in the old manor-house, and he was known by every one in the village. Son succeeded father in manor, farm-

MOOR HALL, HUMPHRIES END, NEAR STROUD, GLOUCESTER

house, and cottage, and the relationship of landlord to tenant, employer to labourer, was intimate and traditional. Agricultural depression has told heavily on the race of old squires. Times are changed. Young squires love the excitement of towns and travel. The manor-house is often closed or let to strangers, and village life is different now from what it was a century ago.

But the manor-house remains, though frequently it is used as a farm-house, and has lost its ancient prestige. It forms a charming feature in the landscape. It is old and weather-beaten, set in a framework of pines and deciduous trees, with lawns and shrubberies. Look at the beautiful illustration of Moor Hall, near Stroud, with its high gables, tiled roofs, and mullioned windows, and compare it with any foreign building of the same size, and you will respect the memories of our English builders. The manor-house at Wool, Dorset, a county very rich in such buildings, is also very attractive, approached by a fine stone bridge, and surrounded by trees and farm buildings.

Most of the old manor-houses have given place to Tudor or Elizabethan structures, but there is a perfect fourteenth-century example at Little Hempton, near Totnes. It consists of a quadrangle with a small central court, into which all the windows, except that of the hall, look from sunless rooms. The hall was heated by a brazier in the centre—at least, the heat might have been sufficient to thaw numbed fingers. A gloomy parlour with a fire-place in it, kitchen, porter's lodge, cellar, and stable, and upstairs one long dormitory complete the building, which was none too comfortable.

Some villages have two manor-houses, and others were divided into several manors. In Berkshire, at Sutton Courtney, there are two houses—one formerly attached to the abbey of Abingdon, the other to the Courtney family. The great feature was a large hall; at one end was an entrance

THE MANOR-HOUSE AND BRIDGE, WOOL, DORSET

passage separating the hall from the buttery or store-room, and above this the ladies' bower. A chapel was also attached, sometimes placed at one end of the loft above the hall. From this elementary plan subsequent manor-houses have been developed.

The tradition of the central hall lingered on for centuries, and can be seen still in manor-house, farmstead, and cottage.

FARM-HOUSE NEAR KNOWLE, WARWICKSHIRE

The central hall with wings at each side, and barns and stables and cow-sheds completing a quadrangle—this was the ideal plan of the squire's house, and yeoman-farmer and cottagers copied the buildings of their betters. The illustration of the farm-house near Knowle, Warwickshire, is picturesque in every detail, and shows the maintenance of the tradition of the central hall. Sometimes there is only one wing, as in the view of the beautiful old farmstead at Sutton Green, Oxfordshire, roofed with thatch and covered with creepers. The half-timbered farm-house at Rowington, Warwickshire,

FARM-HOUSE, SUTTON GREEN, NEAR STANTON HARCOURT, OXON

is an old dwelling of early date, probably about the sixteenth century, which has the same original plan, but has taken to itself an addition at some later period.

It is beyond our purpose to sketch the growth of domestic architecture and trace the evolution of the modern mansion

FARM-HOUSE, ROWINGTON, WARWICKSHIRE

from the Saxon hall. But there are many old farm-houses in England, once manor-houses, which retain, in spite of subsequent alterations, the distinguishing features of mediæval architecture. The twelfth century saw a separate sleeping-chamber for the lord and his lady. In the next century they dined in a room apart from their servants.

This process of development led to a multiplication of

rooms and the diminution of the size of the great hall. The walls were raised, and an upper room was formed under the roof for sleeping accommodation. In smaller houses, during the fifteenth century, the hall disappears, and corridors are introduced in order to give access to the various chambers. Some of these houses are built in the form of the letters E and H, which fanciful architectural authorities interpret as the initials of Henry VIII and Queen Elizabeth. But the former plan is merely a development of the hall with wings at each end and a porch added, and the H is a hall with the wings considerably extended.

The beautiful Tudor and Elizabethan manor-houses and palaces built at this time, when English domestic architecture reached the period of its highest perfection, are too grand and magnificent for us who are considering humbler abodes. But the style of their construction is reflected in the farm-houses and cottages. We see in these the same beautiful gables and projecting upper storeys, the same lattice casements, irregular corners and recesses which present themselves everywhere, and add a strange beauty to the whole appearance. Such common features link together the cottage, farm, and manor-house, just as the English character unites the various elements of our social existence and blends squire, farmer, and peasant into one community with common feeling and interests and a mutual respect.

The old rectory is an important house in the village, and ranks next to the manor-house. It is usually a picturesque building, and several fourteenth-century parsonages remain, though some have been so altered that only small portions of the old house exist. Mediæval parsonages survive still at West Dean, Sussex; King's Stanley and Notgrove, Gloucestershire; Wonstone, Hants; Helmsley, Yorkshire; Shillingford, Berks; and at Alfriston, Sussex. This last example follows the usual type of fourteenth-century house, and consists of a fine hall, the lower part divided off by a screen, a solar of two storeys at one end, and a kitchen at the other. It is built of oak framework, filled in with wattle and daub. These old houses show that the duty of entertaining strangers and travellers was duly recognised by the clergy. There were rooms set apart for guests, and the large stables attached to rectories and vicarages were not for the purpose of providing accommodation for the rector's hunters, but for the steeds of his visitors.

The interior of the rectory speaks of learning and books. Books line the walls of the study ; they climb the stairs ; they overflow into dining-room and drawing-room. The light that shines from the study window is always there. Country-folk retire early to bed, and the village lights are soon extinguished ; but that study light is always burning far into the night, and is scarcely put out before the approach of dawn calls the labourer from his couch to begin his daily toil.

IV

COTTAGE ARCHITECTURE

THE building of beautiful cottages is almost a lost art, if we may judge from the hideous examples which modern builders are accustomed to rear amidst beautiful scenery that claimed exemption from such desecration. "Cottage-building does not pay," is the dictum of both farmer, squire, and jerry-builder. "You cannot get more than two per cent on your money spent in erecting dwellings for the poor." Hence people are accustomed to build as cheaply as possible, and to destroy the beautiful earth and many a rustic paradise by the erection of these detestable architectural enormities. It has been said that villas at Hindhead seem to have broken out upon the once majestic hill like a red skin eruption. There is a sad contrast between these unsightly edifices with their glaring brick walls, their slate roofs, their little ungainly stunted chimneys, and the old-fashioned thatched or tiled dwellings that form so charming a feature of English rural scenery.

With the aid of our artist we hope to visit many of the humbler examples of English domestic architecture. It is well that they should be sketched, inspected, admired, and noted at once, as year by year their numbers are decreasing. Every year sees the destruction of several of these old buildings, which a little care and judicious restoration might have saved. Ruskin's words should be writ in bold big letters at the head of the bye-laws of every District Council :—

"Watch an old building with anxious care ; guard it as best you may, and at any cost, from any influence of dilapidation. Count its stones as you would the jewels of a crown. Set watchers about it, as if at the gate of a besieged city ; bind it together with iron when it loosens ; stay it with timber when it declines. Do not care about the unsightliness of the aid—better a crutch than a lost limb ; and do this tenderly and reverently and continually, and many a generation will still be born and pass away beneath its shadow."

COTTAGES AT WINSON, GLOUCESTERSHIRE (COLN VALLEY)

If this sound advice had been universally taken many a beautiful old cottage would have been spared to us, and our eyes would not be offended by the wondrous creations of estate agents and local builders who have no other ambitions but to build cheaply.

COTTAGE ARCHITECTURE

How different are the old cottages of England. Here is an admirable description of an ideal rural dwelling written more than a century ago :—[1]

"I figure in my imagination a small house, of odd, irregular form, with various harmonious colouring, the effects of weather, time, and accident, the whole environed with smiling verdure, having a contented, cheerful, inviting aspect, and a door open to receive a gossip neighbour, or weary, exhausted traveller. There are many indescribable some-things that must necessarily combine to give to a dwelling this distinguishing character. A porch at entrance ; irregular breaks in the direction of the walls, one part higher than the other ; various roofing of different materials, thatch particularly, boldly projecting ; fronts partly built of brick, partly weather-boarded, and partly brick-nogging dashed ; casement window lights, are all conducive and constitute its features."

Such is a cottage which the poet and the painter loves, a type which is happily not extinct in modern England—

> Its roof with reeds and mosses covered o'er,
> And honeysuckles climbing round the door ;
> While mantling vines along its walls are spread,
> And clustering ivy decks the chimney head.

Its garden is rich with old-fashioned English flowers, and amongst them we notice roses, pansies, peonies, sweet-williams, and London Pride, which flourish in the herbaceous borders that line the approach to the cottage door. It is set in a framework that enhances its beauties. Dark woods form the background. In front there is the village green, the centre of the amusements of old village life, whereon children are seen disporting themselves ; the old church is nigh at hand with its lofty spire. Other graceful dwellings cluster round the green, and the rude pond, wild hedgerows, and irregular plantations complete the picture.

[1] *An Essay on British Cottage Architecture*, by James Malton, 1798.

THE CHARM OF THE ENGLISH VILLAGE

Of such a cottage the poet sings :—

> Close in the dingle of a wood
> Obscured with boughs a cottage stood;
> Sweetbriar decked its lowly door,
> And vines spread all the summit o'er;
> An old barn's gable end was seen
> Sprinkled with nature's mossy green,
> Hard on the right, from whence the flail
> Of thrasher sounded down the vale—
> A vale where many a flow'ret gay
> Sipt a clear streamlet on its way—
> A vale above whose leafy shade
> The village steeple shews its head.

Such is the pleasing picture of a rural home, the peculiar, beautiful, and picturesque feature of English rural scenery, where dwell

> Those calm delights that ask but little room.

The illustrations show many such a gem of cottage architecture gathered from many counties. The builders of these used no alien materials. They built surely and well with substances best suited for their purpose which the neighbourhood afforded. Stone, timber, flint, all were made to serve their purpose. In the region of good stone quarries of Gloucestershire and Somerset we find the beautiful cottages at Winson, and the charming bay in a cottage at Montacute. This latter house, with its armorial bearings carved beneath the upper window, has doubtless seen better days, and was probably a house of some pretensions. Kent and Essex, where good building stone is scarce, furnish fine examples of half-timbered cottages.

It is interesting to notice how these timber houses were built. The materials were inexpensive and easily procurable. The surrounding woods supplied plenty of oak timber, and earth and sand, straw or reeds were all that was needed. Sometimes a solid foundation of stone or brick was built in order to protect the woodwork from the damp earth, and on this were placed horizontal beams. At the corners of the house very stout upright posts were erected, which were formed from the trunk of a tree with the root left on it, and

A COTTAGE BAY, MONTACUTE, SOMERSET

placed upward, this root curving outwards so as to form a support for the upper storey. A curious and important feature of these old houses is their projecting storeys. I have never heard a satisfactory reason given for this strange construction. I can understand that in towns where space

BRENCHLEY, KENT

was scarce it would have been an advantage to be able to increase the size of the upper rooms, but when there was no restriction as to the ground to be occupied by the house and land was plentiful, it is difficult to discover why our fore-fathers constructed their houses on this plan. Possibly the

PART OF A HOUSE AT NEWPORT, ESSEX

fashion was first established of necessity in towns, and the traditional mode of building was continued in the country. Some say that by this means our ancestors tried to protect the lower part of the house from the weather; others with some ingenuity suggest that these projecting storeys were in-tended to form a covered walk for passengers in the streets, and to protect them from the slops which the careless housewife of Elizabethan times cast recklessly from the upstairs windows. Projecting upper storeys are not earlier than the reign of Elizabeth. Their weight necessitated a strong foundation.

We have constructed our foundations, horizontal timber base, and corner posts, the roots of the trunks being cut into brackets both on the outside and inside of the

POUNDSBRIDGE, KENT

house. These strong and massive angle-posts were often richly carved and moulded. Other upright posts were erected along the base about seven feet apart. These horizontal timbers were fastened, socketed, or mortised into the upright beams so as to form square openings, which were divided into smaller squares by less stout timbers. Then the foundations of the floor of the upper rooms were constructed by beams laid across the tops of the upright beams. The floor of this upper section of the house pro-

GREAT CHESTERFORD, ESSEX

jected about two feet beyond that of the lower. Sometimes the projection was confined to one or two sides of the houses, but frequently it extended on all the sides. The upper storey was constructed in an exactly similar fashion, and the timbers of the roof were then placed in position. Usually beams

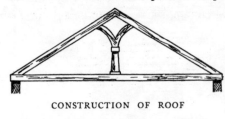

CONSTRUCTION OF ROOF

spanned the upper storey, and at their centre an upright post, called a " king-post," was erected, which supported a cross-beam which was held in position by braces and fastened at the ends to the slanting beams of the roof.

A pleasing characteristic of some of the Kent cottages and farm-houses is the sunken central bay. The two outer bays have projecting upper storeys ; the central bay has not. The eaves of the roof extend the whole length of the building, and that portion over the central bay is supported by curved braces.

Mr. Ellis, a practical and experienced craftsman, suggests[1] there were three types of these half-timbered houses, to which he has given the names Post and Pan, Transom Framed, and Intertie Framed work. Frequently these types are varied and sometimes combined in the same building. The Post and Pan style is the earliest, and consists of a post and a panel placed alternately and equally spaced. Upright posts were placed between the horizontal ground sill and the head-beam which supported the roof, the spaces between these vertical posts being filled with clay or wattle and daub. These posts at first were fixed close together, but by degrees the builders obtained confidence, set their posts wider apart, and held them together by transoms. This led them to adopt the Transom Frame construction, the walls being now

[1] In *Modern Practical Carpentry*, by George Ellis (Batsford, 1906).

composed of vertical and horizontal timbers forming larger square or oblong openings. Some of them were used for doors and windows, and the others filled in with interlaced hazel-sticks covered with plaster or with brick-nogging. In order to strengthen the framework straight or curved beams were introduced at the angles, the latter being formed from the large limbs of trees sawn in two. Intertie Framework was a kind of reversal of the Transom style. Strong uninterrupted horizontal beams were its foundation, the vertical posts being framed between them. Much skill and ingenuity were displayed in the decorating of the panels.

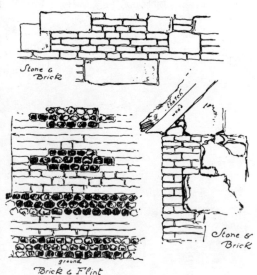

VARIETIES OF WALLING FROM HANTS
AND DORSET

A good example of cottages built in the manner which I have described is given in the illustration of the houses at Brenchley, Kent (p. 52), a county famous for its half-timbered dwelling-places. We notice the overhanging upper storey, the upright timbers placed close together, a sign of early building, the sunken central bay, tiled roof, and the little dormer windows jutting out therefrom, which break the long expanse of roof and add to its picturesqueness. The portion of the house shown in the illustration is built in three bays. A bay was the standard of architectural measurement, and houses were sold or let by the bay. A bay measured roughly sixteen feet, and was the length required in farm buildings for the standing of two pairs of oxen. The view of part of the cottage at Newport, Essex (p. 53), shows a very fine example. The complete house is an early example of the Kentish type of sunken central bay, as already described (p. 56), of which the upper storey projects considerably beyond the lower. The upright timbers placed

BRICK AND FLINT COTTAGES, READING STREET, KENT

close together again point to an early date, and it will be noticed that the interstices are filled in with thin bricks or tiles arranged in herring-bone fashion, like the stones of Saxon buildings.[1] There is a cottage at Lyme Regis where this arrangement is seen, and in Kent there are numerous instances of this pleasing variety. The grey oak and the red brick harmonise well together. Flint and stone in

[1] Herring-bone work was formerly considered a characteristic of Saxon architecture, but it can be seen also in Norman walls.

MANSELL LACY, HEREFORDSHIRE

chequered squares are not uncommon in the latter county. The panelled window in the upper storey of the Newport cottage retains some Gothic features, and beneath it there is a curious carving of a king and queen sitting and startled by the strains of a celestial choir. One angel is playing on a harp and the other apparently on an organ.

Another fine Kentish example is shown, a cottage, now an inn, at Poundsbridge (p. 54). The initials of the builder are recorded, and also, happily, the date of its construction, 1593. It is an excellent example of a half-timbered house. The cottage at Great Chesterford (p. 55) is remarkable for the elaborate decoration of the plaster which was accomplished in 1692, and is probably later than the house itself. This ornamentation is called Pargetting, to which we shall refer again presently.

The appearance of our cottages has been much altered since they left the hands of the sixteenth-century craftsman. One peculiarity of the oak timbers is that they often shrink. Hence the joints came apart, and being exposed to the weather became decayed. In consequence of this the buildings settled, and new methods had to be devised in order to make them weatherproof. In order to keep out the rain the villagers sometimes, especially in Surrey, hung the walls with tiles which have various shapes, a common one being semicircular. Artists love to depict these tile-hung houses, to which age imparts a beautiful colour. Other methods for preserving these timber-framed cottages were to cover them with deal boarding or to plaster the walls. Hence beneath an outer coating of tile or plaster or boards there remains an old timber-framed house, the construction of which we have tried to describe.

The mortar used in these old buildings is very strong and good. An old poet tells of

> The morter is maked so well,
> So mai no man hit breke
> Wiz no stele.

ABBOTS MORTON, WORCESTERSHIRE

In order to strengthen the mortar used in old Sussex and Surrey houses and elsewhere, the process of "galleting" or "garneting" was adopted. The bricklayers used to decorate the rather wide or uneven mortar joint with small pieces of black ironstone stuck into the mortar. "Galleting" dates

HINXTON, CAMBRIDGESHIRE

back to Jacobean times, and is not to be found in sixteenth-century work.

There is often a great variety of walling in the southern counties. Stone is combined with brick and brick with flint in a remarkable manner. Examples of this are shown in our illustrations (p. 57), noticed by our artist in Hants and Dorset. At Binscombe there are cottages built of rough Bargate stone with brick dressings. In the neighbourhood of

Petworth you will see brick used for the label-mouldings and strings and arches, while the walls and mullions and doorways are constructed of stone. Our artist has sketched some remarkable examples of brick and flint cottages at Reading Street, Kent (p. 58).

COTTAGE PORCH, UPTON SNODSBURY, WORCESTERSHIRE

Sussex houses are often whitewashed and have thatched roofs, but sometimes Horsham stone is used. This stone easily flakes into plates like thick slates, and forms large grey flat slabs on which "the weather works like a great artist in harmonies of moss, lichen, and stain. No roofing so combines dignity and homeliness, and no roofing, except possibly thatch (which, however, is short-lived), so surely passes into

63

the landscape."[1] It is to be regretted that this stone is no longer used for roofing. The slabs are somewhat thick and heavy, and modern rafters are not adapted to bear their weight. If you want to have a roof of Horsham stone, you can only accomplish your purpose by pulling down an old house and carrying off the slabs. Perhaps the small Cotswold stone slabs are even more beautiful. Like the Sussex stones,

COTTAGE AT BEAULIEU, HANTS

these "Stonesfield slates," as they are called, have unfortunately fallen into disuse for new buildings, but a praiseworthy effort is now being made to quarry them, and again render them available for building purposes. Old Lancashire and Yorkshire cottages have heavy stone roofs which somewhat resemble those fashioned with Horsham slabs.

Very lovely are these country cottages; peaceful, pic-

[1] *Highways and Byways in Sussex*, by E. V. Lucas.

turesque, pleasant, with their graceful gables and jutting eaves, altogether delightful. What could be more charming than that view of a group of cottages at Mansell Lacy, Herefordshire (p. 59), in its framework of dark trees, or the old half-timbered house at Abbots Morton, Worcester-

MARSTON SICCA, GLOUCESTERSHIRE

shire (p. 61). Even the flat, monotonous country of Cambridgeshire is relieved by picturesque humble dwellings such as those drawn by our artist at Hinxton (p. 62).

We have seen several examples of tiled roofs. An old English red-tiled roof, when it has become mellowed by age with moss and lichen growing upon it, is one of the great charms of an English landscape.

Nothing shows better the skill and ingenuity of the old builders than the means they adopted to overcome peculiar difficulties. The roofs of cottages usually slope steeply in order that the rain may flow off easily. But these Sussex masons found that the heavy Horsham slates strained and dragged at the pegs and laths, and fell and injured the roof. So they decreased the slope of the roof, and the difficulty was obviated. However, as the rain did not flow off very

COTTAGES AT GREAT TEW, OXON

well, they were obliged to use cement and stop with mortar.

There is a great variety in old ridge-tiling, but the humbler abodes usually have simple bent tiles or the plain half-round as a finish to the roof.

The ends of the gables are often adorned with barge-boards. A simple but effective example is shown in the illustration of the cottage porch at Upton Snodsbury, in Worcestershire, on page 63. Early examples have their edges

cut into cusps, or pierced with tracery in the form of trefoils
or quatrefoils. In Jacobean times the builders placed a finial
at the ridge and pendants at the eaves, and the perforated
designs were more fantastic. Even poor-looking houses have

THATCHING AT CODFORD ST. PETER, WILTSHIRE

elaborately carved or moulded bargeboards. In old houses
the bargeboards project about a foot from the surface of the
wall. In the eighteenth century, when weather-tiling was
introduced, the distances between the wall and the bargeboards was diminished, and ultimately they were placed flush

with it. Elaborately carved boards were discarded, and the ends of the gables moulded.

The most picturesque mode of roofing is thatch, and its glories and beauties have often been sung by poets and depicted by artists. It is charming in its youth, maturity, and decay. Thatch is not so usual as it was formerly. Good

CALBOURNE, ISLE OF WIGHT

straw is not so plentiful. Farmers grow less corn, and the straw broken by thrashing machines is not so good for thatching as that thrashed by the flail. The skill of the old thatcher produced most artistic effects. The author of an article on the "Old Thatched Rectory" bids us to

"notice the exquisitely neat finish of the roof-ridge, the most critical point of the whole : the geometrical patterns formed by the spars just below, which help, by their grip, to hold it in its place for years : the faultless symmetry of the slopes, the clean-cut edges, the gentle curves of the upper windows which rise above the 'plate'; and, better still, the embrace which, as with the encircling arms of a mother, it gives to the deep-planted, half-hidden dormer window in the middle of the roof, nestling lovingly within it, and by its very look inviting to peacefulness and repose. Note, too, the change of colouring in the work as time goes on; the rich sun-set tint, beautiful as the locks of Ceres, when the work is just completed; the warm brown of the succeeding years; the emerald green, the symptom of advancing age, when lichens and moss have begun to gather thick upon it; and 'last scene of all, which ends' its quiet, un-eventful history, when winds and rain have done their work upon it, the rounded meandering ridges, and the sinuous deep-cut furrows, which, like the waters of a troubled sea, ruffle its once smooth surface."[1]

CAVENDISH, SUFFOLK

The varied beauties of thatch are well seen in the illustrations. Notice the lovely cottage at Beaulieu (p. 64), with its thatch encircling the little dormer windows and the beautiful curves of the roof. The humbler dwelling·at Marston Sicca (p. 65) has a finely wrought thatch ingeniously extended to embrace the shed. Great Tew has the credit of

[1] "The Old Thatched Rectory and its Birds" (*Nineteenth Century*), by R. Bosworth Smith.

BURWASH, SUSSEX

being one of the prettiest villages in England. It lies amongst the steep, well-timbered hills in Mid-Oxfordshire. All the cottages are built of a local stone, which has turned to a grey yellow or rich ochre, and are either steeply thatched or roofed with thinnish slabs of the same yellowish grey stone, about the size of slates, and called by the vulgar " slats." The illustration (p. 66) shows some of these delightful dwellings. The diamond-paned windows have stone mullions with drip-stones over them, and over the doors are stone cornices with spandrels. No one cottage repeats another. There is no slate or red brick in the village. Honeysuckle, roses, clematis, ivy, japonica beautify the cottage walls, in front of which are bright, well-kept gardens behind trim hedges. The old stocks still stand on the village green, as they stood when Lord Falkland rode from his home here to fight for King Charles and die at the battle of Newbury.

Other examples of thatched cottages are shown : a gracefully shaped thatch at Codford St. Peter (p. 67), a street of Isle of Wight cottages at Calbourne (p. 68), and the charming little dormer window of a cottage at Cavendish, Suffolk (p. 69).

Burwash is a pretty Sussex village in a region famous for good cottages. It has memories of smugglers, of a genial rector who wrote a book about Sussex folk and Sussex, and of a learned poetical curate who became Professor of Poetry at Oxford. Our artist has given us a sketch of the village street with its broach-spired church. The house on the right is superior to the others, and possesses the appearance of a Queen Anne building. It was built in 1699, and has inside some fine plaster-work, with gracefully modelled birds, over the staircase.

V

DETAILS, DECORATION, AND INTERIORS OF COTTAGES

THERE is much else that may be noted in the details of cottage architecture which deserves to be recorded. Our village builders were not content to leave the humble dwellings bare and unadorned, but loved to add to them ornamental details such as their good taste suggested. This is especially noticeable in the decoration of the plaster-covered panels framed by the timbers that formed the framework of their houses. The men of the seventeenth century set themselves to embellish that which we moderns are content to leave perfectly blank. Pargetted work and plaster work are especial features of timber-framed houses. The usual method was to press the plaster into a concave mould and then transfer it to the plastered surface when still moist. Our artist has made some sketches of these external plaster details taken from houses in Hertfordshire, Essex, and Suffolk. It is well that all such pargetting work should be carefully drawn and recorded, as much of it is fast perishing or being destroyed. Some simple examples found in Berkshire are shown (p. 75). These consist simply of straight or circular lines, and no pressing frame or special apparatus was required for their production; but the effect is produced by the contrast of rough-cast and smooth plaster, and shows the pride which the builders took in their work and their endeavour with ordinary tools to produce some attempt at ornamentation.

They loved also to stamp their work with their initials,

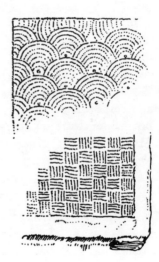

EXTERNAL PLASTER DETAILS (PARGETTING) FROM HERTS,
ESSEX, AND SUFFOLK

and very many houses have carved in stone the date of their construction and the initial letters of the names of the

builders. Heraldic arms also are sculptured on the fine stone buildings in the regions of good quarries, and we give an illustration of a good coat-of-arms found on a house at Winchcombe, whence the famous "Jack of Newbury," the rich clothier of Henry VIII's time, derived his family name. Over the door of a substantial house at Stanton-in-the-

Winchcombe

Peak, Derbyshire, we see the initials " E. G. L." with the date 1664 (p. 76). It is a fine door worthy of a mansion, with its flight of steps and handsome tympanum and hood-moulding. There is much dignity and solid work about many of these cottage doors. They retain the Gothic spirit, with their Tudor arches and Perpendicular hood-moulding. Possibly the doorways at Croscombe (p. 77) and

Marston Magna, Somerset (p. 79, formerly a window) are early sixteenth-century work, and belong to buildings which have seen better days.

Cottage doors are always open and invite us to enter. We may still see ingle-nooks and open fireplaces. Our artist has discovered some charming examples of these attractive features. That one at Garnacott, near Bideford (p. 78), is very characteristic with its cauldron and kettle and dogs. A beam runs along the top of the fire-place, stretching across the opening from which a short curtain hangs. This represents the typical kind of cottage fire-place which is already rare and is rapidly becoming extinct, for though picturesque, it does not commend itself to the modern housewife, who greatly prefers the iron "kitchener" or range for her cooking. This example shows the old cloth above the mantelpiece, and the seat and rush-bottomed chair in harmony with the rest of the fittings. Above this is a shelf blackened by the smoke of ages whereon some of the cottager's treasures repose, kettles and cooking-pots, and possibly modern nicknacks, cups bearing inscriptions "A Present from Brighton"

PARGETTING IN BERKSHIRE

or "For a Good Girl," in conjunction with impossible milkmaids, shepherds, and shepherdesses, and dogs and cats with great staring eyes, and miniature dolls' houses, and mugs and pigs of divers patterns. The window at the back of the fire-place is curious, and is occasionally found opening out of the ingle-nook. Frequently these old fire-places communicate with a small oven built out from the house. This is often semicircular and ingeniously roofed with tiles or slates. It was a custom almost universal in former times for the cottagers to bake their own bread, and it is still practised in remote districts, such as Shropshire and in the Welsh hills, where even modern cottages are sometimes built with ovens.

STANTON-IN-THE-PEAK, DERBYSHIRE

Miss Jekyll has made a wonderful collection of objects discovered in country cottages in West Surrey, and has presented them to the museum of the local archæological society at Guildford. Her book *Old West Surrey* is a faithful and valuable guide to the contents of cottages. She has found cooking implements pierced with crosses, which probably came from some monastic house, and countless objects far too numerous to mention. Our illustration of the Marston Magna inglenook (p. 80) shows a good specimen of the chimney-crane and hanger, which exhibit the splendid work of the local blacksmith. The crane turns on its pivot. The hanger moves along the top bar of the crane, and can be raised or lowered, and on its hook rests the kettle or cooking-pot. One of our

COTTAGE DOORWAY, CROSCOMBE, SOMERSET

illustrations reveals the primitive method of illumination, the rushlight, which was used long after the dawn of the nineteenth century. Rushes were peeled and then drawn through melted grease, and then left to dry. The rushlight holders have a movable jaw at the top and a fixed one. The movable jaw has a knob at the end. In one of the illustrations given this knob has been converted into a candle-socket. Many are the other curious implements which old cottages disclose.

We glance at a delightful window in the quaint old town of Burford (p. 81). I dare not call it a village, though it is but a small place ; but it has had a great history, and is one of the most picturesque

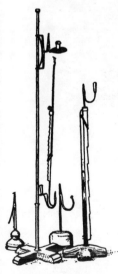

RUSHLIGHT HOLDERS

COTTAGE FIRE-PLACE, GARNACOTT (NEAR BIDEFORD), NORTH DEVON

and interesting little towns in England. That "windowed niche" looks very attractive with its mullions set in a curved bay. Not less lovely is the cottage window at Spratton, Northants (p. 82), viewed from outside, adorned with comely creepers, stone mullions, and diamond panes ; and there is an interesting cottage window at Sutton Courtney, Berkshire (p. 82), which is of a classical Renaissance character, and makes us wonder how it managed to get into this rather remote Berkshire village.

COTTAGE DOORWAY, MARSTON MAGNA, SOMERSET

A great deal may be said about farm-house and cottage chimneys, their construction and development. An immense amount of ingenuity was exercised in their construction. In the older houses there is often a great central chimney, and all the flues are placed together, crowned by the shafts. A good example is shown on page 69. The builders did not aim at utility alone, but strove to add beauty and diversity by using moulded bricks, numerous angles and projecting courses. The thinness of the old bricks and the thickness of the mortar assisted them in producing a picturesque effect.

The most common form of cottage chimney is that which is placed at the end or side of a house, and is usually a large structure. If the broad part reaches above the height of the ceiling of the ground floor you will probably find a bacon-loft, wherein some sides of bacon are being smoked. The chimney, beginning with its straight upright base, has a steep slope, sometimes covered with tiles, then another

MARSTON MAGNA, SOMERSET

straight piece, then an arrangement of brick steps, repeated again until the chimney is ready for its shaft with its projecting courses, and finished with a comely pot, or a "bonnet" fashioned of red tiles. Great pains was often taken to adorn the head, and the effect is wonderfully fine, the means employed natural and simple and unaffected.

A COTSWOLD
GABLE FINIAL

The illustration (p. 79) shows the stack of a Cotswold cottage retaining traces of

80

Gothic influence. It has an octagonal shaft pierced with quatrefoil openings and the remains of a pyramidal roof.

A COTTAGE WINDOW, BURFORD, OXON

The chimney cornices in the Cotswolds often have elaborately decorated architrave and frieze, enriched with sunk

 patterns, raised diamonds or other devices. The whole district abounds with grand stone-built houses, beautiful types of building, simple yet strong, which owe their origin to the wealth

A COTTAGE WINDOW, SPRATTON, NORTHANTS

and skill of the great clothiers and woolmen who flourished here in olden days. We admire their fine stone porches and four-centred arched doorways, the curious and splendidly wrought iron-work of hinge and latch, handle and casement-fasteners, the mullioned bay and oriel windows with their lead lattice glazing and diamond panes, the decorated gables, and many other attractive features. A whole chapter would not record all their beauties, and the reader who seeks additional information is referred to Mr. Dawber and Mr. Davie's book on the *Old Cottages, Farmhouses, and other Stone Buildings in the Cotswold District*, wherein he will find all that he needs.

We have lingered perhaps too long amid the cottages, and must now pass on to observe other interesting features of our village.

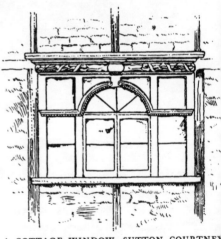

A COTTAGE WINDOW, SUTTON COURTNEY BERKSHIRE

VI

VILLAGE GARDENS

WE have some noble gardens in our village. The squire's garden was once visited by that great garden-lover, John Evelyn, who states that "the gardens and waters are as elegant as 'tis possible to make a flat by art and industrie and no meane expense, my Lady being extraordinarily skill'd in the flowery part, and my Lord in diligence of planting." He praises the delicious and rare fruit, the fine timber, and goes on to tell of the garden "so beset with all manner of sweete shrubbs that it perfumes the aire. The distribution also of the quarters, walks, and parterres is excellent; the nurseries, kitchen-garden full of the most desirable plants ; two very noble orangeries, well furnished, but above all the canall and fish ponds . . . in a word all that can make a country seate delightful." Happily this beautiful garden has escaped the devastation of such wretches as Capability Brown, Kent, and such desecrators, who in cultivating the taste of landscape gardening destroyed more than half the old gardens in England, and scarcely left us a decent hedge or sheltered walk to protect us from the east winds.

The old rectory garden is worth visiting, with its fine terrace, and paths sheltered with high and thick box hedges, herbaceous borders, and old trees. Utility mingles itself with beauty, and the kitchen-garden blends itself with the flower-beds wherein many old English plants find a home. The grouping for colour effect is especially noticeable in this moderately sized garden, which tells that the rector or his lady are not unskilled in floriculture.

But the cottage gardens constitute one of the chief charms of the village. They show what wonderful results can be obtained on a small plot of ground with simple flowers. It was Charles Dickens who said that " in the culture of flowers there cannot, by their nature, be anything solitary or exclusive. The wind that blows over the cottage porch sweeps over the garden of the nobleman, and as the rain descends on the just and on the unjust, so it communicates to all gardens, both rich and poor, an interchange of pleasure and enjoyment."

Poets in many ages have sung sweetly of the beauty of our cottage gardens, and none more sweetly than the late Poet Laureate, who tells their praises thus :—

> One look'd all rose tree, and another wore
> A close-set robe of jasmine sown with stars ;
> This had a rosy sea of gilliflowers
> About it ; this a milky way on earth,
> Like visions in the Northern Dreamer's heavens,
> A lily avenue climbing to the doors ;
> One, almost to the martin-haunted eaves,
> A summer burial deep in hollyhocks ;
> Each its own charm.

When we return from visiting other lands, we notice with gratified eyes these wayside homely gardens, which are peculiarly English. Englishmen have always loved their gardens, and all classes share in this affection. It is not so with other European nations. You do not find abroad those flowers in cottage windows cherished so carefully through the winter months ; you do not see the thrifty Frenchman or German stealing from his potato ground or onion bed a nice broad space for the cultivation of flowers. Whereas in England you will scarcely find a cottage garden that is not gay and bright with beautiful flowers, or the

A COTTAGE GARDEN, TRENT, DORSETSHIRE

poorest labourer, however large his family may be, willing to sacrifice the plants in which he takes so great a pride.

At all seasons of the year these cottage gardens look beautiful. Snowdrops and crocuses seem to rear their heads earlier in the springtime in their village plots than in the gardens of the great. Yellow and purple crocuses are there, and then a little later dogtooth, white and purple violets, and yellow daffodils. My villagers have given me bunches of violets long before they grew in the rectory garden, save those Neapolitan ones that flourish in a frame. Primroses transplanted from the neighbouring woods are not despised. A few stray tulips begin to show themselves, immensely prized by the cottager, and soon the wallflowers are in bloom filling the air with beautiful scent, and forget-me-nots reflect the blueness of the sky. Villagers love the simple polyanthus, and soon on the wall of the cottage is seen the red japonica in full flower. Then the roses come into bloom, and many a cottage can boast of its fine Gloire de Dijon or Maréchal Niel or strong-growing crimson rambler. Clematis plants of various hues are seen on many a cottage wall, and ivy "that creepeth o'er ruins old" loves to cling to rustic dwelling-places, and sometimes clothes walls and thatch and chimney with its dark green leaves. The honeysuckle is a

A GARDEN ENTRANCE, CHALE-GREEN, ISLE OF WIGHT

favourite plant for climbing purposes. It covers the porch and sheds its rich perfume around, nor in the warmer parts of England is the vine unknown.

The southern counties of England afford the most luxuriant examples of cottage gardens which form a con-

COTTAGE GARDEN ENTRANCE, STRETTON SUGWAS, HEREFORDSHIRE

spicuous charm of our villages. Our artist discovered a delightful old garden at Trent, Dorset (p. 85), wherein countless flowers have found a home and give a glowing patch of colour to the landscape. The Isle of Wight with its warm climate abounds in beautiful gardens. The illustration of a garden entrance at Chalegreen looks inviting, and we should like to mount the steps shaded by luxuriant yew and see all that lies beyond. We know of another beautiful little garden

at Shalfleet in the island, where there is a charming well-
trimmed edging of box which surrounds a little path and
central bed, wherein stocks and a carefully tended standard rose
raises its beautiful head. Cottage garden paths are usually

SOUTH WARNBOROUGH, HANTS

made of gravel. In Sussex they are paved with large flat
Horsham slabs of stone. Box-edgings are not uncommon,
than which nothing can be more handsome or suitable.

Nor are the flowers confined to the garden. You will
scarcely find a cottage that has not some plants in the window
which are tended with the greatest care, and are watered
and washed so religiously that they flourish famously.

A COTTAGE ENTRANCE, SULGRAVE, NORTHANTS

The favourite flowers for window gardens are geraniums, hydrangeas, fuchsias, an occasional cactus or begonia, musk and balsam, and many others which obscure the light of day and make the cottage dark, but the peasant cares not for that if he can see his flowers.

Old-fashioned flowers are the chief charm of the cottage garden, and are prized by the true garden-lover far higher than bedding-out plants or the ordinary annuals. Nowhere do they flourish better than in the peasant's rustic pleasure-ground. As the summer advances we see the lilacs and laburnums, sweet-williams and tall white Madonna lilies, gillyflowers and love-lies-bleeding, the larkspur and the lupin, pinks and carnations, the ever-constant wallflowers, and the Canterbury bells. The everlasting-pea is ever welcome in its cottage home, and dahlias are greatly prized, not the single ones so much as the old-fashioned, tight-growing formal kinds.

Hardy annuals have in some rural gardens ousted the old-fashioned flowers. Nasturtiums and china-asters and stocks flourish where once the sweet-william and other herbaceous plants were regarded with delight. We hope that the rustics will return to their first love, and cherish again the old flowers which are the true glory of a rustic garden.

Cottagers, though expert gardeners, are very often puzzled by the foreign names assigned to flowers, especially to roses, which they dearly love, and which are the chief glory of our gardens whether they be large or small. The roses themselves would scarcely know their names when pronounced by our villagers, so strangely transformed and Anglicised are they. Thus the villagers twist the Gloire de Dijon into "Glory to thee John," and the rose named after the great rose-grower, Dean Reynolds Hole, is called Reynard's Hole. General Jacqueminot becomes in popular nomenclature General Jack-me-not, and the bright crimson Géant des

Batailles becomes Gent of Battles. But the roses bloom no less beautifully on account of this murdering of their names.

The old favourite roses which you find in these gardens

APPLETON, BUCKS

are the Sweetbriar, the Cabbage, the York and Lancaster, the Moss, the old White Damask, the double white, brother of the pretty pink Maiden's Blush. But some cottagers are more ambitious, and obtain cuttings of many varieties of modern rose trees, and hybrids and Teas now flourish in the peasant's border as in the lord's rosarium. The love of this flower is indeed the "one touch of nature which makes the whole world kin."

Examples of the formal garden may be seen as we walk along our English roads. Box trees cut into fantastic shapes and clipped yews are occasionally met with. The trees are made to assume the appearance of peacocks with long flow-

CUT HEDGE AND THATCHED VERANDAH, ACTON TRUSSEL, STAFFORDSHIRE

ing tails or other strange shapes, and awkward figures of men and animals. Happily the fashion of clipping and hacking trees is not universally followed, and except in some districts is rare in cottage gardens. In the country of West Herefordshire this practice is common, and there is a well-known example in the garden of the cottage just outside Haddon Hall. In the view of a cottage garden entrance at Stretton Sugwas, Herefordshire, on page 87, we see a very fierce peacock with flowing tail endeavouring to reach across the path to peck some food from a cylindrical-looking vessel on the opposite side. The trees are admirably clipped. And at South Warnborough, Hants, our artist has discovered some good examples of fantastic clipping (p. 88). The cottage entrance in the village of Sulgrave, Northants (p. 89), guarded by two stately cypresses, is very imposing, and the raising of the garden above the road with the flight of steps worthy of a rustic Haddon Hall romance adds to the effect. At Appleton the cottage entrance is overshadowed by two yew trees growing into one large mass (p. 91), a curious example of differing treatment when we compare it with the Northamptonshire example. A third example, again quite distinct in its arrangement and yet equally attractive, is the pretty cut hedge and thatched verandah at Acton Trussel, Staffordshire, in which the space under the sweeping cut hedge is further shaded by large round shrubs ; a spot very shady in summer and sheltered in winter.

Here is a description of a Berkshire village garden told by one who knows her county well and the quaint ways of her rural neighbours. She tells of the glories of

"the Red House which gained its title in its youth. A century of wear and weather has toned the bricks until they look almost colourless by contrast with the rich, crimson flowers of the pyrus japonica that is trained beneath the lower windows. The upper portion of the walls is covered by a vine, among the yellowing leaves of which hang, during autumn, tight bunches of small purple grapes that supply the wherewithal for grape wine. At one side of the narrow, railed-in space separating the front door from the street, stands an old pear tree, loaded every season with fruit which, owing to its 'iron' quality, escapes the hands of boy-marauders. The little spot reflects all the tints of the rain-bow save in the depth of winter. The first buds to pierce the brown earth and brighten its dull surface are such tender blossoms as the snowdrop, hepatica, and winter aconite. To them succeed crocuses, hyacinths, tulips, the scale of colour mounting ever higher as the season advances, until it culminates in a blaze of scarlet, blue, and yellow, that to be fully appreciated should flame against grey, venerable walls or light up the dark sweep of some cedar-studded lawn. The square garden behind the house slopes to the brook near the bridge, and is shut in on two sides by high mud walls half hidden beneath manes of ivy. Along the stream—bordered just there by willows—is a broad band of turf flanked by nut bushes that shelter each a rustic seat, and sparkling in spring with clumps of daffodils tossing their heads in sprightly dance. When the sun is shining through their golden petals and burnishing the surface of the water, when it is brightening the pink willow-buds and revealing unsuspected tints in the mossy trunks of the apple-trees beyond the brook, that little strip of grass is a joy, the remembrance of which abides throughout the year, until the changing months make it once again something more than a memory.[1]

Cottage gardens, of course, combine utility with beauty, and are sorely missed when our rustics, attracted by the glamour of the town, desert the country in order to seek their fortunes in the busy city. The loss of their garden is one of the first steps in their rude awakening. Much else might be written about the attractions of our gardens, whether large or small ; but enough, perhaps, has been told of their beauties and perfections which form so characteristic and charming a feature of English village life.

---

[1] This garden is in the village of West Hendred, Berks, and is described by Miss Hayden in her book *Travels Round Our Village*.

VII

INNS, SHOPS, AND MILLS

AN important house in every village is the inn—a hostel such as Izaak Walton loved to sketch, "an honest alehouse where we shall find a cleanly room, lavender in the windows, and twenty ballads stuck about the wall, where the linen looks white and smells of lavender, and a hostess cleanly, handsome, and civil." Perhaps our village, if it lies along one of the old coaching roads, has more than one such hostelry, and the "Blue Lion" frowns on the "Brown Bull," and the "Raven" croaks at the "Bell." Once they were large and flourishing inns, but their glory has departed. When coaches rattled through the village these inns had a thriving trade, and imagination pictures to our minds the glowing life of the coaching age. We see again the merry coach come in, the "Mercury," or the "Regulator," or the "Lightning," according to the road we choose or the age in which we are pleased to travel. We see the strangely mixed company that hangs about the door, the poor travellers trying to thaw themselves before the blazing hearth, the good cheer that awaits them—huge rounds of beef, monstrous veal pies, mighty hams, and draughts of good old English ale brewed in yon ruined brewhouse, and burgundy and old port. The present landlord can produce, perhaps, some bread and cheese and a glass of ale—that is all ; and one solitary nag stands in the stables where then there was stabling for fifty

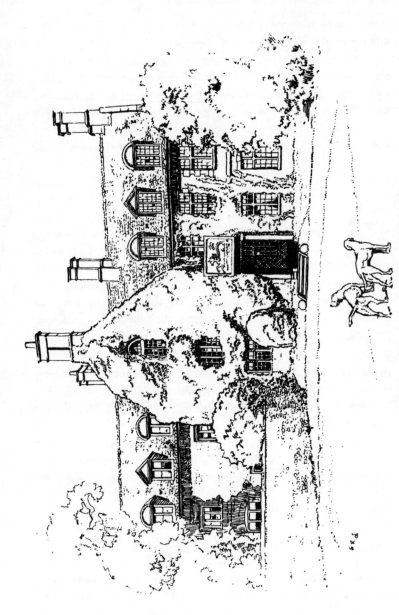

THE SEA HORSE INN, DEANE, NORTHANTS

horses, and the grass grows green in the stable-yard, and silence reigns in the deserted chambers.

But even in their decay how picturesque these old inns are. The red-tiled roof, the deep bay window, the swinging signboard, the huge horse-trough, the pump and outdoor settle, form a picture which artists love to sketch ; while within the old-fashioned fire-place, with seats on each side in the ingle-nook, and the blazing log fire in the dog-grate, are cheering sights to the weary traveller. In his travels in search of the picturesque our artist has found many such inns, and some of them he has sketched. There is the fine old inn at Deane, Northants, with the quaint sign the " Sea Horse." What the sea-horse is doing in the centre of England is not very evident, unless heraldry can help us to a conclusion. The old house at Croscombe, Somerset (p. 98), was formerly the First and Last Inn, a coaching hostel, now no longer needed. Its every detail is charming, and before it races the water over a fine stone mill-dam. Two charming interiors our artist has given us, the Union Inn at Flyford Flavel (p. 99), with its open fire-place into which a modern grate has been inserted, the old-fashioned settle and corresponding details ; and the kitchen of an old Bedfordshire inn (p. 101), which has the unusual well in one corner, that has not yet given way to a pump.

The signboard that swings outside the inn has many stories to tell as it creaks in the wind. Some of these signs are remarkable for the exquisite ironwork that supports them and tells of the skill of the village blacksmiths of former days. The man who forged such beautiful specimens of ironwork had the heart and mind and hand of the true artist, though he were but a simple village blacksmith. The signs, too, at least the old ones, are well painted, and some are constructed of carved wood. A finely carved bunch of grapes, of eighteenth-century work, hangs before the Red Lion Inn at Milford, Surrey, and a study of signs

Sydney R Jones
1907

AN OLD HOUSE (FORMERLY THE FIRST AND LAST INN)
AND MILL DAM, CROSCOMBE, SOMERSET

THE UNION INN, FLYFORD FLAVEL, WORCESTERSHIRE

shows that there must have been a large number of skilful carvers of this bold kind of work about a hundred and fifty years ago. They had plenty of opportunity for exercising their art, as signs were not confined to inns. Unless our artist has improved the swan and the bull (see page 103), the old art of sign-painting has not quite disappeared. There is one inn in England which can boast of a signboard painted by two Royal Academicians, the "St. George and the Dragon" at Wargrave. Mr. Leslie, R.A., and Mr. Broughton, R.A., used to stay at the inn sometimes when they were on sketching bent, and requited the landlord for his attention by repainting his sign. St. George appears on one side regaling himself with a tankard on his way to fight the dragon, and on the other the hero-saint is refreshing himself after the combat. One of the most extraordinary signs in England is shown on page 103. The inn is the "Fox and Hounds" at Barley, Hertfordshire, and the sign is a pack of hounds hunting a fox, followed by two huntsmen. The whole history of sign-boards invites digression, but space forbids a repetition of what I have tried to tell before in another book that deals with the antiquities of English villages, and not so much with their outward charm.[1]

Near the inn stands the shop of the blacksmith, who is a very important person in the village community. We have seen some specimens of his forefathers' work, and though I question whether he could fashion such delicate and ornate supports for signboards, such wonderful ornamental ironwork, he is a very clever "all-round" man. He not only can shoe horses, but repair all kinds of agricultural implements, mend clocks, cut hair, and even in olden days he used to draw teeth. Our village blacksmith is a most accomplished person, and can turn his hand to anything. The village blacksmith has been immortalised in verse, and

---

[1] *English Villages*, by P. H. Ditchfield (Methuen & Co.).

"THE KITCHEN WELL," BEDFORDSHIRE

THE CHARM OF THE ENGLISH VILLAGE

a picture of his smithy drawn by a skilful hand. Longfellow's
poem is so familiar that it need not be quoted.

Still the light of the forge gleams out in the dusk of a winter's
day, and the children try to catch " the burning sparks that
fly like chaff from a thrashing-floor." " Henry Moat, R.S.S.,"
who works at Sturry, Kent (see page 104), is a very up-to-
date smith, and his shop is spruce and neat, unlike most
village smithies, where all sorts of old iron is scattered about,
and where sometimes you may find some curios and treasures.

The village shop is a wondrous place wherein you can buy
anything from a bootlace to a side of bacon. Sweets for
children, needles and thread for the busy housewife, butter
and cheese, tea and ginger-beer—endless is the assortment
of goods which the village shop provides. Whiteley's in
London can scarcely rival its marvellous productiveness.
Very old and quaint is the building. There is one at Ling-
field, Surrey, which has performed its useful mission since
the fifteenth century. It has a central recess with braces
to support the roof-plate. Formerly there was an open
shop-front with wooden shutters hinged at the bottom of
the sills, on the tops of the stall-boards, and which could
be turned down in the daytime at right angles with the
front, and used for displaying wares. In some cases there
were two shutters, the lower one hinged in the bottom sill,
as I have described, while the upper one was hinged to the
top, and when raised formed a pent-house roof. Shake-
speare alludes to this arrangement when he says, in *Love's
Labour's Lost*, " With your hat pent-house like o'er the shop
of your eyes." The door was divided into two halves like
a modern stable door.

Village industries are fast dying out, if they are not all
dead and buried. In the olden days when the cloth trade
was flourishing in Berkshire each village was alive with busy
industrial enterprise. Each cottage had its spinning-wheel,
and every week the clothiers of Reading and Newbury used

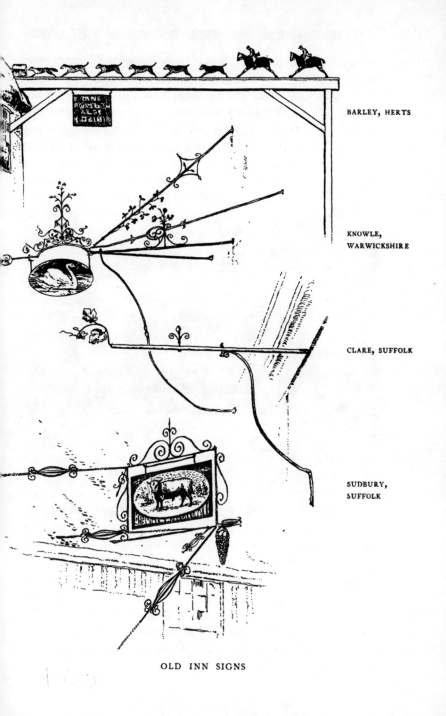

BARLEY, HERTS

KNOWLE, WARWICKSHIRE

CLARE, SUFFOLK

SUDBURY, SUFFOLK

OLD INN SIGNS

to send out their men among the villages, their packhorses laden with wool, and every week they returned, their pack laden with yarn ready for the loom. We give a view of the village of East Hendred, which was a prosperous clothing centre. There is a picturesque field near the church where terraces still remain, which were used for drying cloth, and

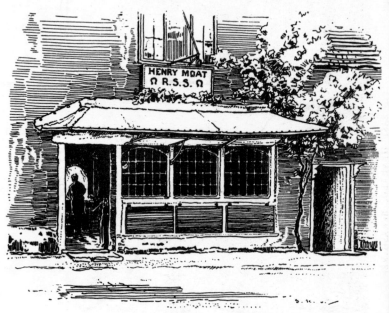

THE BLACKSMITH'S SHOP, STURRY, KENT

a piece of land called "Fulling Mill Meer," where—so Mr. Woodward, who was rector in 1759, stated—"ancient people remembered the ruins of a mill in the stream hard by." This fulling mill was held of the king by John Eston, whose descendant is still lord of the manor. In the church are brasses to the memory of Henry and Roger Eldysley, "mercatores istius ville," and of William Whitway, "pannarius et lanarius." The village had also a flourishing fair, which was held on the downs, and reached from Scutchamore

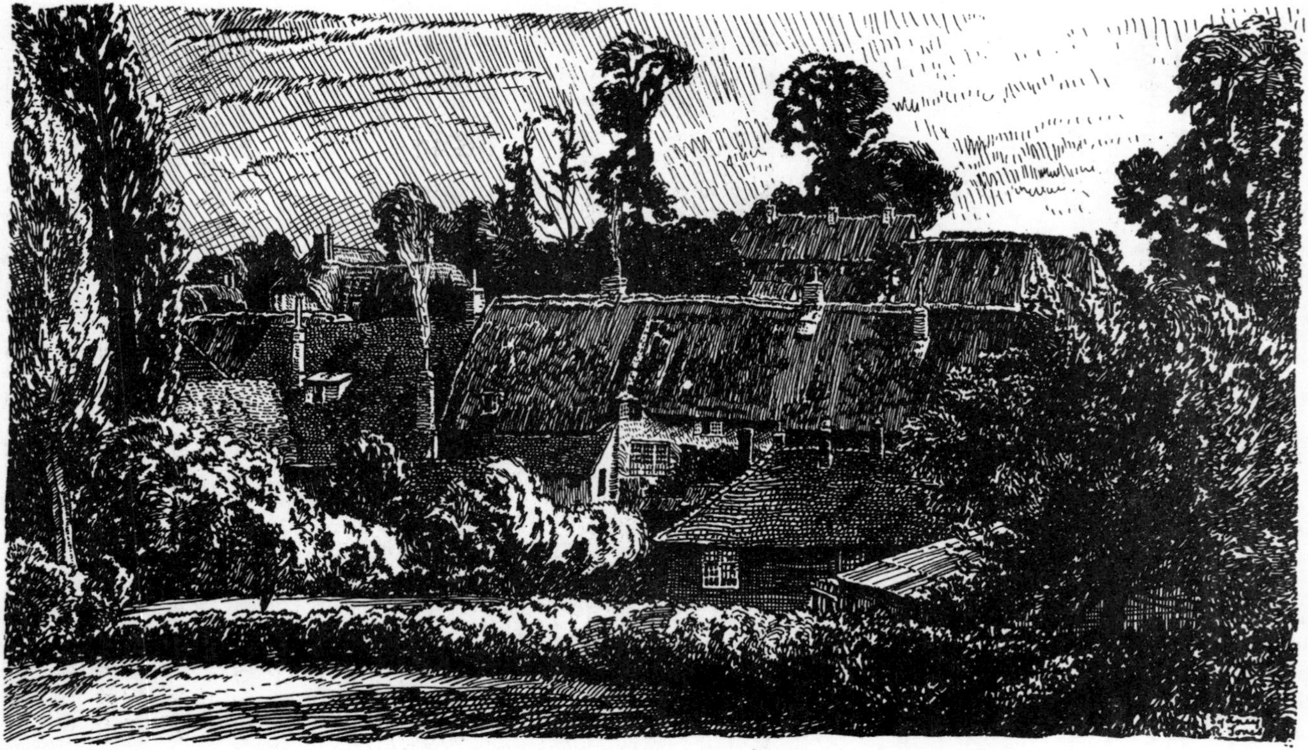

EAST HENDRED, BERKSHIRE

Knob to Hendred, along a straight green road once known as the Golden Mile. It was abolished by James I in 1620. All this testifies to the importance of this little village in former days, and of the flourishing manufacture of cloth carried on there.

But the introduction of machinery, the invention of spinning jennies, carding machines, and like inventions, and the activity of the northern clothiers, turned the tide of fortune elsewhere and killed the village industry. Other trades have suffered in the same way. Gloves were made in many a village in Worcestershire; lace in Buckinghamshire, where the industry has been revived, and in Devonshire, and old dames might have been seen at the cottage doors with their bobbins and pillows and "earned good money" by their deft fingers.

The mill still stands, but it is a ruin, picturesque in its decay. The overshot-wheel is still and lifeless, with rotting timbers unhidden by pent-house or roof.

"No wains piled high with corn roll heavily down the lane to disgorge swollen sacks to fill its gaping vats. The corn laws, the cheap loaf, 'which came as a gift to us poor folks,' killed the mill in the valley. Its business declined; chains became rusty; doors and windows fell out and the roof fell in; the stream was diverted by a side cut, and the great oaken wheel hung rotting on its pin."[1]

It is one of the oldest houses in the village, and once one of the most important. It was the lord's mill, the mill owned by the lord of the manor, and to it all the tenants were obliged to bring their corn to be ground, unless they would undergo divers pains and penalties. But it is a ruin now; its glories are departed; its millstones adorn the squire's garden; but it still adds beauty to the scene. The stream that once turned the great floats rushes calmly by, but its banks are the home of many ferns and flowers, and the weir is still a picturesque miniature cascade. Some

[1] *Travels Round Our Village*, by Miss Hayden.

ASHFORD IN THE WATER, NEAR HADDON HALL, DERBYSHIRE

water-mills still survive—" cool and splashing homes—homes of peaceful bustle," as Mr. Lucas happily describes them—and the miller with his white hat is not quite dead, a pleasing personage in the village community. If old songs are to be trusted, he was always "jolly," "hearty," "hale and bold," especially if he lived by the river Dee, where

> He worked and sang from morn till night,
> No lark more blithe than he ;

and mightily independent, caring for nobody as nobody cared for him. We cannot afford to lose such a sturdy, jovial character.

The village once had other mills that derived their power not from the stream but from the wind, and in East Anglia these windmills still remain, relics of the age ere steam had begun to exercise its relentless sway. Our artist has given a sketch of that at Ballingdon, Essex, a typical windmill with its sloping boarded sides, its imposing cap, and giant sails that woo the wind. Sussex also has its windmills standing high and white, things of life and beauty, suitable for the grinding of the golden harvest of the fields, not ugly, noisy *infernos* like the steam-mills. Artists have loved to depict our windmills, especially Constable, than which there are no more charming features in an English landscape. Many have disappeared in recent years, but the name "Windmill Hill" often records their site and preserves their memories.

Though many of our village industries are dead, we have others still very much alive. Besides the usual agricultural occupations, ploughing and sowing, digging, reaping, and thatching, we have our skilful woodmen who can fell and carry the largest trees with consummate ease, and it is a wonderful sight to see them roll these massive giants of the forest up the slides to the great wood-wagons, and the horses are as skilful as the men. Broom-squires still make

AN ESSEX MILL, BALLINGDON

birch and heath brooms, and are a rough race. Two of
them met at Newbury market and exchanged confidences :

"Jack, I can't tell 'ow thee sells the brooms so cheap like.
I steals the ling, I steals the butts, I steals the withies ; but I
can't sell 'em as cheap as thee."

"Why," said his companion unblushingly, "I steals 'em
ready made."

Hop-growing, cider-making, chair-making, straw-plaiting,
and many other industries still live on, and it would be well
if others could be introduced, in order to add to the pros-
perity and relieve the monotony of ordinary rural existence.

VIII

ALMSHOUSES AND GRAMMAR SCHOOLS

IN many villages there are old almshouses founded by pious benefactors for "poor brethren and sisters," God's hostels, where men and women on whom the snows of life have begun to fall thickly, may rest and recruit and "take their ease" before they start on their last long journey. Here the tired and the moneyless find harbourage. Some of these houses are quite humble places erected by some good squire for the aged poor of the village ; others are large and beautiful buildings erected by some great noble or rich merchant, or London City Company, for a wider scheme of charity. Scattered over the country we find these delightful resting-places. We enter the quiet courtyard paved with cobble stones, or, as it is at Wantage, with knuckle-bones, relics of the town's former industry of tanning, and see the panelled dining-hall with its dark oaken table, the chapel where daily prayer is said, the comfortable little rooms of the brothers and sisters, the time-worn pump in the courtyard, the flowers in the garden beds and in the windows, and we are glad these old folks should have so sweet a home as they pause before their last long journey. Our illustration shows the pretty village of Ewelme, with a row of cottages half a mile long, which have before their doors a sparkling stream dammed here and there into water-cress beds. At the top of the street on a steep knoll stand church and school and almshouses of the mellowest fifteenth-century bricks, as beautiful and structurally sound as the

EWELME, OXFORDSHIRE, SHOWING THE ALMSHOUSES AND SCHOOL BELOW THE CHURCH

pious founders left them.[1] These founders were the unhappy William de la Pole, first Duke of Suffolk, and his
good wife the Duchess Alice. The Duke inherited Ewelme
through Alice Chaucer, a kinswoman of the poet, and "for
love of her and the commoditie of her landes fell much to

THE ALMSHOUSES, AUDLEY END, ESSEX

dwell in Oxfordshire," and in 1430–40 was busy building
a manor place "of brick and Tymbre and set within a fayre
mote," a church, an almshouse, and a school. The manor
place, or "Palace," as it was called, has disappeared, but the
almshouse and school remain, witnesses of the munificence
of the founders. We need not follow the fate of the poor

[1] *History of Oxfordshire*, by J. Meade Falkner.

duke, favourite minister of Henry VI, who was exiled by the Yorkist faction, and beheaded by the sailors on his way to banishment. Twenty-five years of widowhood fell to his bereaved duchess, who finished her husband's buildings, calling the almshouse "God's House," and then reposed beneath one of the finest monuments in England in the church hard by.

Near where I am writing is the beautiful almshouse called Lucas's Hospital, founded by Henry Lucas for the old men of several parishes in the neighbourhood, and placed in the charge of the Drapers' Company of the City of London. It is a fine Jacobean house of red brick with tiled roof and two wings. The Quainton almshouses are very picturesque and quietly impressive, built in 1687 by Richard Winwood. The building has eleven gables and four blocks of chimneys, and each inmate has two rooms opening out of each other, a porch with seats, and a little garden attached.

Our illustrations show the beautiful almshouses at Audley End, Essex, an architectural gem, and the more imposing hostel at Corsham, with its great porch and immense coat-of-arms. It was built in 1663, and consists of six houses with a cloister, master's house, and free school, retaining some good woodwork.

Nor did our pious benefactors forget the youth of the village and the needs of education. It is the fashion for short-sighted politicians to suppose that all education began in the magical year 1870, and to forget all that was done before to teach the youths of our village. The teaching given in the old dame schools at the beginning of the last century was defective enough. We hear of one of the best conducted by a blind man, who taught fairly well, but was rather interrupted in his academic labours by being obliged to turn his wife's mangle. A good dame confessed, "It is not much they pay me, and it is not much I teach them." The curriculum of another school was described by its mis-

THE ALMSHOUSES, CORSHAM, WILTSHIRE

tress : " I teach them to read and to sew, and the Belief and the Commandments, and them little things." And yet their scholars did not turn out so badly. Most of them can read ; writing is a little difficult, and they prefer, when required to sign their name to a will or marriage register, to plead incapability and to make their mark ; but the women who

EARDISLAND, HEREFORDSHIRE
The house in the centre was formerly the Grammar School

were taught in these schools can sew far better than girls can now, and the men can do wonderful sums in their minds, especially when these concern their wages. But I am describing the old schools that existed in some of our villages, not simple elementary schools, but grammar schools, secondary schools, where the boys learned Latin. Many of them are called Edward VI's grammar schools, but were really established long before the Reformation. Some three hundred schools were in existence before 1535, some of them taught by chantry priests, or by a schoolmaster provided by a guild, or by a master of a hospital or almshouse. Duchess Alice at Ewelme founded a school which appears in our

PORCH OF THE OLD GRAMMAR SCHOOL, WEOBLEY, HEREFORDSHIRE (BUILT BY JOHN ABEL)

sketch (p. 112). Childrey is a very small Berkshire village, but its smallness did not prevent William Fettiplace founding a free grammar school there in 1526, in which poor children could be taught elementary subjects and richer folk Latin. The founder's will is too long to quote, but he lays down strict rules for teaching. Moreover, the chaplain-school-master was not allowed to " keep or breed hunting birds or to hunt regularly." A good old-fashioned grammar school is shown in the view of Eardisland, Herefordshire, and in the same county there is an old grammar school at Weobley, the porch of which is beautifully designed and proportioned. It was built by John Abel, the master of Jacobean timber work. This porch is enriched with some quaint carving typical of the period. Many years have passed since the building was used for a school, but it has undergone very little change during the two and a half centuries of its existence. It stands in a small town famous for its half-timbered houses (p. 3). John Abel was the most famous architect of his time, a native of Sarnesfield, who built market houses at Leominster (now preserved as a private residence, see p. 157, where the vane is illustrated), Kington, and Brecon, the grammar school at Kington, and restored the roof of Abbey Dore church, and did much else that is worthy of his name. His tombstone exists in the churchyard at Sarnesfield, where he was buried in 1674, aged 97, showing the figure of himself and his two wives and the emblems of his profession—compasses, square, and rule. Some of his creations have escaped the decay of time, but been destroyed by the hand of the vandal. May the good folk of Herefordshire prize and preserve all the remaining work of this great artist.

IX

VILLAGE CROSSES, GREENS, AND OLD-TIME PUNISHMENTS

IN many villages still stands the village cross, a picturesque object, often headless and dilapidated, but remarkable for its interesting associations and old-time records. Some stand in churchyards, others adorn the village green or open space where markets were once held; and there are others standing lonely by the wayside, or that marked the boundaries of ancient monastic properties. Each tells its own story of the habits, customs, and modes of worship of our forefathers. Time has dealt hardly with these relics of antiquity. Many fell before the storm of Puritanical iconoclastic zeal in 1643, when the Parliament ordered the destruction of all crucifixes, images, and pictures of God and the saints. The crosses in London were levelled with the ground, and throughout the country many a beautiful work of art which had existed hundreds of years shared the same fate.

The earliest crosses were those erected in churchyards, of which that at Tong, Salop, may be taken as an example. Its steps are worn by the rains and frosts of centuries. This cross preserves the memory of the first conversion of the Saxon villagers to Christianity. There are many Saxon crosses still existing, and some of them have beautiful carving and scrollwork, which tell of the skill of Saxon masons, who with very simple and rude tools could produce such wonderful specimens of art. The crosses at Whalley, Ruthwell, Bewcastle,

TONG, SALOP

Eyam, Ilkley, Hexham, Bishop Auckland, are all curiously carved with quaint designs, proclaiming much symbolical teaching, and were set up before churches were built by Wilfrid, Paulinus, and other saints who first preached the Gospel to the Saxon people.[1] There are several others in Somerset : Rowberrow, Kelston, and West Camel are Saxon ; Harptree, Norman ; Chilton Trinity and Dunster, early thirteenth century ; Broomfield, late thirteenth century ; Williton and

THE MARKET PLACE, SOMERTON, SOMERSET

Wiveliscombe, early fourteenth century ; Bishops-Lydiard and Chewton Mendip, late fourteenth century ; and Wraxall, fifteenth century.

Market crosses are another class, and are found in large villages in which markets were held by royal grant to some great landowner or monastery. These were called "cheeping" crosses, from the Anglo-Saxon word *cheap*, to buy, from which Cheapside, in London, Chippenham, and Chipping Norton derive their names. The earliest form of a market cross was a pillar placed on steps. Later on their

[1] An account of these crosses is given in *English Villages* (Methuen & Co.).

height was increased, and niches for sculptured figures were added. Religion was so blended with the social and commercial life of the nation that sacred subjects were deemed not inappropriate for the place of buying and selling in a market-place. They reminded people of the sacredness of bargains. Subsequently they were enclosed in an octagonally shaped penthouse, wherein the abbot's servant or the reeve

THE OLD MARKET HOUSE, PEMBRIDGE, HEREFORDSHIRE

of the manor-lord received the market dues. The market cross at Somerton, Somerset, was built in 1670. It has three steps and some curious gargoyles at the weather-string angles. Numerous other examples exist in the same county. We give an illustration of the old market house at Pembridge, Herefordshire, but no cross exists there now. Markets were held in churchyards until the end of the thirteenth century; hence the churchyard crosses would often be used as market crosses.

SHAPWICK, DORSET

CHILDS WICKHAM, GLOUCESTERSHIRE

VILLAGE CROSSES AND GREENS

As I have said, countless villages have their crosses, though they had no markets. They stand on the village green or in the centre of the village nigh the church. It was the central station for the processions when the villagers perambulated the village at Rogation-tide. Preaching friars harangued the people standing on its steps. Penitents were ordered to make their pilgrimages barefoot, scantily attired, to the cross, which was sometimes called the Weeping Cross, and there to kneel and confess their sins. Fairs were held around it, which were originally of a sacred character, and were held on the festival of the saint to whom the church was dedicated. Many associations cluster round this old village cross. Our illustrations show the battered cross at Shapwick, Dorset (p. 122), and that at Childs Wickham, Gloucestershire. The steps and base of this are ancient, but the urn-shaped top is probably a later addition. Lymm, in Cheshire, has an elaborate cross, and near it are the village stocks, concerning which we shall have more to say presently (p. 126).

Wayside crosses are less numerous than other kinds of crosses. Many have been destroyed. Some have been removed from their lonely stations and others pulled down, the stones being used for gate-posts. An old book published in 1496 explains their object : "For thys reason ben croysses by ye waye than whan folke passinge see ye croysses they shoulde thynke on Hym that deyed on ye croysse above al thynge." They are like a Calvary in a French village, and were erected for a similar purpose. Crosses were sometimes set to mark the spot where the bodies of illustrious persons rested during their journey to their last resting-place. Such were the Eleanor crosses that were set up by Edward I at the places where the body of his beloved queen rested on the way to Westminster. They formed a good boundary mark for monastic property, as on account of their sacred character few would dare to disturb them. Curious legends cluster round these crosses. There is one near Little Bud-

CROSS AND STOCKS, LYMM, CHESHIRE

SEVENHAMPTON, GLOUCESTERSHIRE

worth, Cheshire, which is gradually sinking into the earth. According to the prophet Nixon, when it quite disappears the end of the world will come. It is getting near the ground; we do not wish to cause our readers unnecessary alarm.

Hard by the cross is the village green, the scene of the

DINTON GREEN, BUCKS

old village games and revels, where the May-pole was raised and the rustics danced around. Here the old games and bouts of quarter-staff and back-sword play took place; here the English bowmen learned their skill, and the Whitsun rejoicings were celebrated—

A day of jubilee,
An ancient holiday,
When lo! the rural revels are begun,
And gaily echoing to the laughing sky
O'er the smooth-shaven green,
Resounds the voice of mirth.

VILLAGE CROSSES AND GREENS

Our artist has given sketches of the characteristic greens at Sevenhampton, Gloucestershire, and the Buckinghamshire greens at Penn and Dinton. We should like to linger in these villages and inspect the interesting church at Dinton

THE POND, TYLER'S GREEN, PENN, BUCKS

and the old manor-house with its pictures and curios and its associations with Simon Mayne the regicide, and to see the house of the Penn family, but want of space will not allow of this digression.

In the sketch of Tyler's Green there is shown the village pond which in some cases was the scene of rural justice.

At the end of the pond in olden times was a long plank which turned on a swivel, with a chair at one end. This machine was fastened to a frame which ran on wheels, and when justice had to be administered it was pushed to the edge of the pond. It was called a ducking-stool, or "cuck-ing-stool," and was used to duck scolds or brawlers. The

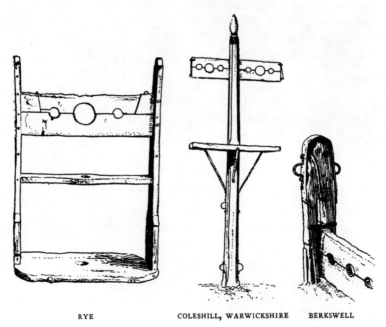

RYE   COLESHILL, WARWICKSHIRE   BERKSWELL

PILLORIES, STOCKS, AND WHIPPING-POSTS

culprit was placed in the chair, and the other end of the plank was raised several times, so that the ardour of the culprit was cooled by frequent immersions in the cold water of the pond. We give an illustration of the ducking-stool at Leominster, now in the Priory Church.

We have already caught a glimpse of the stocks at Lymm (p. 126). This rude instrument of justice stood on the village green or near the cross, and sometimes beside it, or in conjunction with it, a pillory which held fast the head and arms of the culprit, while the villagers threw stones, rotten eggs, and other missiles at the unhappy victim of rude rustic justice. Two miles from Canterbury is the quaint little town of Fordwich, once a borough and a Cinque Port, now little more than a village. Its town-hall is a quaint building which preserves a ducking-stool. The seats of the old mayor and aldermen are at the far end of the room ; the jury-box is on the left ; the ducking-stool on the central beam ; the prisoner's bar in the centre ; and above you can see

DUCKING-STOOL, LEOMINSTER, HEREFORDSHIRE

the press-gang's drums which used to beat a merry tattoo in the little town when the press-gang came to carry off some poor country lad to serve in H.M. Navy. In a north-country inn there is a sad relic of the story of a pressed man. A young man rode up to the inn with a horse which had cast its shoe, holding in his hand the treacherous shoe. The press-gang were regaling themselves in the hostelry. As he seemed a vigorous youth they seized him. He asked leave to nail his shoe to the beam of the staircase, saying that when he came back from the wars he would come and reclaim it. But he never came, and the shoe hangs there to this day, a sad memorial of a gallant sailor who died for his country in one of Nelson's battles.

One other relic of old times our artist has depicted : the

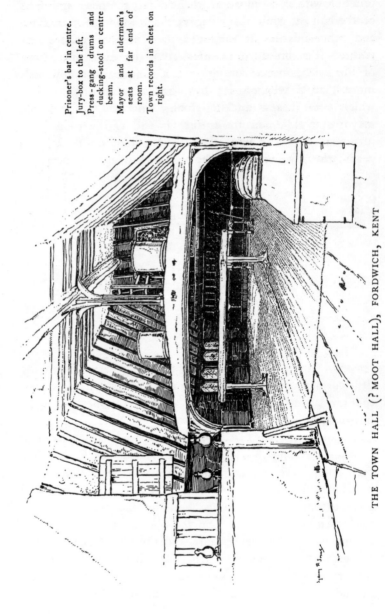

Prisoner's bar in centre.

Jury-box to the left.

Press-gang drums and ducking-stool on centre beam.

Mayor and aldermen's seats at far end of room.

Town records in chest on right.

THE TOWN HALL (? MOOT HALL), FORDWICH, KENT

dread gibbet-irons wherein the bones of some wretched breaker of the laws hung and rattled as the irons creaked and groaned when stirred by the breeze. No wonder our villagers fear to walk to the neighbouring cross-roads, where the dead highwayman or other lawless criminal was hung. It must have been ghostly and ghastly. I am tempted to digress and tell many a story of noted highwaymen, of Bagshot Heath on a moonlight night, of the haunts of the knights of the road, the village inns where they sought refuge and astonished the rustics by their strange tales. I am tempted to tell of their victims, one of whom sang—

GIBBET-IRONS, RYE

> Prepared for war, now Bagshot Heath we cross,
> Where broken gamesters oft repair their loss,

and of the prudent Lady Brown, who readily yielded up her purse to the highwaymen, declaring afterwards to Horace Walpole that she did not mind in the least, "there was nothing but bad money in it. I always keep it on purpose." But hangings and gibbetings thinned the ranks of these notorious highwaymen, and happily the village was freed from the presence of their bodies. The name Gibbet Common remains in some places to remind us of the lawlessness of the past, and museums still preserve these dread irons that once startled poor travellers and kept the rustics to their own firesides after dark.

X

BARNS AND DOVECOTES

A CHARMING feature of a village are the old barns which cluster round the farmstead. The building of great barns has rather gone out of fashion since flails and hand-thrashing became extinct, and we know many new farms which have no barns at all. Perhaps they are not so necessary now as they once were, and modern agriculture does not need them. Be that as it may, the fine old barns are picturesque and attractive buildings, and still have their uses. The grandest of them are the ancient tithe or grange barns formerly attached to some monastery, built in the fourteenth century, as strong as a church and as fine as a minster. Happily many of these mediæval structures have been spared to us, and the village is fortunate which possesses one. In one day's excursion with the Berks Archæological Society we discovered two of them, one of the finest in England at Great Coxwell, and just over the border in Wiltshire the smaller but no less beautiful fourteenth-century barn at Highworth. It is, of course, well known that until the year 1836 all tithes were paid in kind. An old man in Cholsey, Berkshire, remembers the clerk going round the cornfield and placing a peg in every tenth sheaf in order to show that it belonged to the vicar of the parish. All other kinds of grain, hay, wool, peas, beans, etc., were tithed in the same way. Indeed, a woman who had ten children thought she ought to pay tithe, and sent her tenth child to the rector of her parish, who, being a kind-hearted man, accepted the payment of this unusual tithe and brought up the child.

The collecting of tithe in kind necessitated a place in which to store it. Hence tithe barns had to be built, and from mediæval times onwards almost every village had its tithe barn. I am again tempted to digress in order to tell how this system of tithe-paying grew up. It dates back

A BARN AT DOULTING, SOMERSET

to early Saxon times. Even Ethelbert, the first Christian king of Kent, converted by Augustine, allowed a tenth to God, which he called God's Fee, and what was first a voluntary gift for the support of the Church became a legal obligation. It is outside our subject to discuss the origin of tithes. We are inspecting barns, and we understand why tithe barns were needed. The old monasteries had vast estates. They had their own barns near their monasteries; these were not for tithes, but for the produce of their home farms that lay around their monastic house. In other parts of the county or district they had other large estates which they called granges, and on these properties they had grange barns, and each rector or vicar had his tithe barn, which was much smaller than the others. Sometimes the monastery took all the tithe of a parish and had its tithe barn, as at Highworth, and paid back to the vicar something for taking the duty. This was unfortunate, as when the monasteries

BARN AT ARRETON, ISLE OF WIGHT

were dissolved the king and his greedy courtiers took possession of this monastic tithe and only paid the vicar a small stipend, and the Church of England has suffered ever since. More tithe now goes into the hands of laymen than into those of the parochial clergy.

We give an illustration of the fine barn of the abbots of Glastonbury at Doulting, Somerset. It is a grand building, and is of earlier date than most of the great monastic barns, most of which were built in the fourteenth century. This is a fine thirteenth-century structure. The walls are

three feet in thickness, built of the freestone of the neighbouring quarries. It measures 95½ feet by 60 feet, and has
two porches. The buttresses are thick and massive, and
may have been added later than the date of the original
building. The roof is constructed of fine oak, and is covered
with stone slabs. This was a grange barn belonging to
Glastonbury, where there is a noble abbot's barn, built in
1420, cruciform in plan and much ornamented. Our Berkshire barn at Great Coxwell belonged to the Cistercian Abbey
of Beaulieu, and is of immense size. The inside measure-
ments are 152½ feet by 38½ feet, and it rises to a height
of 51 feet to the ridge. The walls are four feet in thickness.
Immense timbers rise from the ground forming piers which
divide the barn into a giant nave with two aisles. There
is a fine porch with a tallat in which the monks are said to
have slept when they came to Coxwell to reap the harvest
on their Berkshire estate. The floor is beaten mud, and
this noble structure is roofed with Stonesfield slate. It is
a grand example of fourteenth-century building. A few
miles away, as I have said, is the Highworth barn, constructed much in the same style but on a smaller scale.

There is a good rectory barn at Enstone, Oxfordshire,
built in 1382 by the abbot of Winchcombe at the request
of Robert Mason, the abbot's bailiff. Shirehampton, near
Bristol, has a large barn which perhaps formerly belonged
to Llanthony Abbey, a picturesque building covered with
creepers. Bredon, Worcestershire; Harmondsworth, Middlesex; Naseby, Northants; Heyford, Oxfordshire; Swalcliffe
and Adderbury, all possess wonderful examples of these
mediæval buildings. Our artist gives us a sketch of a
noble barn at Arreton, in the Isle of Wight, which has a
grandly thatched roof gracefully curved, and a large porch.
Together with the other farm buildings it helps to form a
very picturesque group.

Another additional attraction to the manor-house or

important farm is the pigeon-house or dovecote. Old monasteries and priories also were allowed to have these useful buildings. There is a very fine one at Hurley Priory, Berkshire, and there was a special officer, the *columbarius*, whose duty it was to attend to the pigeons in the dovecote.

PIGEON-HOUSE, RICHARDS CASTLE, HEREFORDSHIRE

This building was erected about the year 1307, and is of great interest. The countless niches, or nests, of chalk within this picturesque old building are very remarkable. It must have held countless birds, but when the prior and convent bargained with John Terry in 1389 to give him a pension including an annual dole of two hundred pigeons, the resources of the dovecote must have been severely taxed.[1]

[1] *St. Mary's, Hurley*, by Rev. F. T. Wethered, 1898.

BARNS AND DOVECOTES

No one but the lord of the manor, the monks, or the rector was allowed to have a pigeon-house, which played an important part in the domestic economy of former days. It provided the only fresh meat that was consumed during the winter months, when the household depended upon salt meat except that which the dovecote supplied, and therefore it was highly prized, carefully stocked, and zealously guarded.

These *columbaria* have not been uninfluenced in their construction by fashion and style. We owe their existence to the Normans, who constructed massive round dovecotes entirely of stone. This style lingered on for centuries. When brickwork was again introduced in the fifteenth century round brick *columbaria* were erected. Half-timbered ones were also fashionable, timber-framed, filled with wattle and daub, and subsequently they assumed hexagonal or octagonal shapes.

Our artist has sketched a picturesque pigeon-house in Richards Castle, Herefordshire. Existing castle dovecotes are rare, but doubtless many were built, as their contents were very useful in case of a siege and during the winter months. I know not whether homing pigeons were ever trained to convey messages to other castles summoning aid for a beleaguered garrison. Rochester and Conisborough Castles have these useful pigeon-houses. There is a good circular dovecote at Church Farm, Garway, Herefordshire, built by the Knights Hospitallers in 1320. Some of these examples are very large, such as the one at South Littleton, which measures eighty-three feet in circumference.[1] In order to reach the nests you climb up a ladder which revolves, and so enables you to reach any particular nest. There are sometimes as many as 1000 nesting-places in these houses, and it must be difficult for a pigeon to discover its own nest some-

[1] "Dovecotes," an article in *Home Counties Magazine*, by Mr. Berkeley, Vol. VII, No. 32.

times if, like humans, birds are ever given to loss of memory. These nesting-places are cunningly devised. The openings are six inches square, and they reach fourteen inches into the

PIGEON-HOUSE AT ODDINGLY, WORCESTERSHIRE

substance of the wall. If the cavity were of the same size throughout its depth the bird would not have room to sit upon her scanty nest; it therefore enlarges, right or left, into an **L**-shaped cavity ten inches in width. The holes are arranged twenty inches apart, in rows, each row being ten inches above the one below. An alighting-ledge projects underneath each alternate tier of holes.[1]

We give an illustration of a dovecote at Oddingly, Worcestershire, a square half-timbered structure which must have furnished shelter for a vast number of birds. It is not so vast as the great dovecote at Lewes, which held 4000 nesting-places, and was as big as a moderate-sized church. It was the property of the monks of the priory, and we may imagine that the possession of such a flock of birds did not endear the reverend brothers to the neighbouring farmers, who were much relieved when the birds and their owners were compelled to fly away. One of the causes of bitternesses which exasperated the peasants of France and brought about the Revolution, was the existence of these vast *columbaria*, the denizens of which preyed upon the cornfields of the poor tenants and peasants and made their farms unproductive.

Many of these dovecotes have disappeared. It is well that they should be preserved as picturesque and pleasing objects, and as memorials of mediæval customs and of the manners of our forefathers.

[1] *Herefordshire Pigeon-houses*, by Mr. Watkins.

XI

OLD ROADS, BRIDGES AND RIVERS

THE story of our English village, its charm and fascination, is incomplete without an account of its roads and trackways. "If you wish to read aright the history of a district, of a city, or of a village, you must begin by learning the alphabet of its roads," wisely observes a writer in *Blackwood's Magazine*. These are the oldest of all ancient landmarks. The position of the village, its plan and boundaries, the story of earthworks, burying-grounds, church and castle, all depend upon the roads. How was their course originally determined? Who first planned them? Perhaps our earliest ancestors followed the cross-tracks by which the wild animals descended from the high ground to the water. Where hard dry roads now run along the river valleys by the beds of streams there was in ancient times marsh or far-spreading overflowing sheets of water. Hence our ancestors followed the natural features of the hills. Our first roads ran along the highest ridges of the hills; subsequently more sheltered ways were sought by the hill-sides. The shallowest parts of the rivers were sought where they could find fords. Trails through the woods became pack-horse roads, were then widened into wagon-tracks, and at last developed into fine smooth roads. Some of the roads by which we travel to-day have been traversed by an infinite variety of passengers. Our Celtic forefathers, their Roman conquerors, Saxon hosts, Norman knights, mediæval merchants and pilgrims to the shrines of St. Thomas of Canterbury or our Lady of Walsingham, the wains of the clothiers piled high with English cloth, gallant cavaliers and the buff-coated troopers of Cromwell, all follow each other in a strange procession along these country roads, and we have seen already the ghosts of the old stage coaches, the " Lightning" and the "Quicksilver," and heard the cheery notes of the post-horn, which were far more melodious than the hoot of the motor-car.

Straight through the heart of the village runs the old Roman road. It was "old" before the Romans came. You can see on the hills around earthworks and camps that guarded this road, and are relics of British tribes and prehistoric races which flourished here long before the Romans came to conquer our island. There is the great Watling Street, Ermine Street, the Icknield Way or the road of the Iceni, ancient trackways of the tribes. High on the Berkshire downs this last road runs, known as the Ridgeway, while below it is the later road, the "Portway," probably British too, but used and improved by the Romans. From the east coast to the west the whole road ran ; Watling Street from Dover through London to the north ; the Fosse and Ermine Street were west-country roads, and there were numerous others. The Romans transformed these British trackways, levelled, straightened, and paved them, and formed new lines of roads leading from one to another of the many stations which they established in all parts of the country. Camden describes the Roman ways in Britain as running in some places through drained fens, in others through low valleys, raised and paved, and we have traversed the famous High Street on the top of Westmoreland hills, and dug a few inches beneath the turf to find the pavement laid by these wonderful people. No wonder the Saxon folk deemed these ways the work of demons or demi-gods, and called the road from Staines to Silchester the Devil's Highway.

Fords were at first used by the Romans for crossing streams and rivers, but these were ill-suited to their requirements, and during their domination the first era of bridge-building set in. So substantial were these structures that through centuries of Saxon and Norman rule they survived and remained in use almost to our own day. After the Norman Conquest, when the country settled down and new towns and villages arose, another period of bridge-building

SONNING ON THAMES, BERKSHIRE

began, which has left us many beautiful examples of architectural art. Their builders were great landowners and merchants, wealthy abbeys, special guilds like that at Maidenhead, which not only erected the bridge but afterwards maintained it, and the corporations of cities and towns. It was considered a religious work, this bridge-building, and a chapel was not infrequently built on the bridge, wherein the traveller could pray for the soul of the kind builder, and seek a blessing on his journey and implore a safe passage across the river. These old bridges have been restored and repaired again and again, but they often retain a considerable part of their ancient structure. The Kentish river Medway is spanned by several of these old bridges. There is the old bridge at Yalding, with its deeply embayed cut-waters of rough ragstone, which have been frequently repaired, but it is substantially the original bridge as it was constructed in the fifteenth century. There is the picturesque bridge at Twyford, Kent; another at Latingford with a buttressed cut-water; another at Teston; and the fine fifteenth-century bridge at East Farleigh, with four ribbed and pointed arches and bold cut-waters of wrought stone.

We give an illustration of the picturesque bridge at Sonning, Berkshire, beautiful in colour, cool and comely in its arches, the subject of many paintings. There are three bridges across the Thames at this delightfully picturesque old village, and parts of them have been already gradually rebuilt with iron fittings, and further demolition is threatened, even if it has not already taken place. Originally these bridges were the glory of the village and date from mediæval times. They are built of brick, and good brick is a material as nearly imperishable as any that man can build with. There is hardly any limit to the life of a brick or stone bridge, whereas an iron or steel bridge requires constant supervision. The oldest iron bridge in this country—at Coalbrookdale, in Shropshire—has just failed after 123 years of life. It was worn out by old age, whereas the Roman bridge at Rimini, the mediæval ones at St. Ives, Bradford-on-Avon, and countless other places in this country and abroad, are in daily use, and likely to remain serviceable for many centuries to come. The increased use of terrible traction-engines of gigantic weight, drawing heavy wagons containing tons of bricks, creates fears in the hearts of the lovers of these ancient structures, and possibly those which lie in the track of these fearsome vehicles will not long resist their onslaughts. They should be ruthlessly forbidden to cross them, and their owners compelled to construct others more suitable to their unwieldy weight. Hideous iron-girder erections are good enough for them.

The lore of old bridges is a fascinating subject. Abingdon has a bridge built in 1389 and connected with the Fraternity of the Holy Cross. The Guild had a Bridge Priest to pray for the souls of the benefactors and founders—John Brett and John Houchens, and Sir Peter Besils who gave the

COLESHILL, WARWICKSHIRE

stone and left houses, the rents of which were devoted to its repair, and Geoffrey Barbour who gave some wealth for the same object. The Guild of St. Andrew and St. Mary Magdalene, established by Henry VI in 1452, maintained the bridge at Maidenhead. It existed as early as 1298, when a grant was made for its repair. The town owes its origin to the bridge, as Camden tells us that after its erection Maidenhead began to have inns and to be so frequented as to outvie its neighbouring mother, Bray, a much more ancient place. The present graceful bridge was built in 1772 from

designs by Sir Roland Taylor. A beautiful old bridge connected Reading and Caversham, and it had a chapel which
contained many relics of saints ; but it has been replaced by
a hideous iron-girder structure. We give a sketch of the
graceful old bridge at Coleshill, Warwickshire, with its six
arches and massive cut-waters. The bridge and river, the

SUNRISE ON THE STOUR AT NAYLAND, SUFFOLK

village street and houses embedded in trees, and the tall spire
of the church, form a beautiful group.

The rivers and streams that flow through or near many
villages add greatly to their charm. In Berkshire we have
our Thames, which poets call "stately" or "silvery," [the
great watery highway traversed by Saxons and then by ruth-
less Danes, who burned the towns and villages along its
banks, and left behind them weapons which are eagerly
sought after by the antiquary. The whole story of the
Thames would fill volumes from the time when it was a
wide-spreading river opening out into large lagoons until

it contracted its bed, and was at last chained and locked and bound, and made to turn innumerable mills and convey securely barges and boats on its comparatively smooth surface. It can still be angry and rage and swell with mighty floods and torrents, but it invites with pleasant smiles the water-idlers on a summer afternoon and the keen oarsmen who love to strive along its course during the greatest regatta of the world. But the smaller and less stately rivers and streams are no less inviting to the lover of nature ; rivers just wide enough for small boats, where you can idle and fish or watch the kingfishers. Such a river is the Stour at Nayland, Suffolk, or the Rother in Sussex, where " one can walk by its side for miles and hear no sound save the music of repose—the soft munching of the cows in the meadows, the chuckle of the water as a rat slips in, the sudden yet soothing plash caused by a jumping fish. Around one's head in the evening the stag-beetle buzzes with its multiplicity of wings and fierce lobster-like claws outstretched."[1] In summer the river that flows through the village looks enchanting with its wealth of lilies, reeds, and rush " with its lovely staff of blossom just like a little sceptre" ; the low riverside meadows that "flaunt their marigolds " ; or in winter, when

> Nipped in their bath the stalk-reeds one by one
> Flash each its clinging diamond in the sun.

Possibly near your village you may find a melancholy long-disused canal. It is now covered with green weeds and overgrown with reeds and rushes. No barge ever tries to make its way along it. Just a hundred years ago it was dug with eager zeal. Thousands of pounds were spent upon it. A network of such canals was made late in the eighteenth and early in the nineteenth century. For a few years they rejoiced in their strength. They connected

---

[1] *Highways and Byways in Sussex*, by E. V. Lucas.

Sydney R Jones

THE FOOTBRIDGE, COUGHTON, WARWICKSHIRE

navigable rivers. Barges laden with coals and goods of all kinds conveyed their treasures to country towns and villages. A roaring trade was done at the wharfs, and all was animation, when the tiresome railways were invented and killed the canal, which remains silent, derelict. It is a pathetic story. Some hopeful people declare they have a great future and may yet be used; but in the meantime they are still, the homes of water-fowl and fish, their banks glorious with reeds and flowers, while bridges and locks are not without a peculiar charm, and afford subjects for melancholy philosophers.

We have traversed the old roads, crossed bridges and, like our village rustics, loved to linger upon them, and watched the river as it flows and the stagnant waters of the canal. Our course takes us homewards to our inn, and we have yet another bridge to cross, a footbridge like that at Coughton, Warwickshire, which Mr. Sydney R. Jones has so cleverly drawn. It does not look very strong and safe, and a heavy man would like perhaps to have a bridge-chapel at its side in order that he might pray for a safe crossing. It is old and shakes terribly as we cross, but we pass in safety, and wander to our resting-place for our last night's sojourn in the village.

XII

SUNDIALS AND WEATHERCOCKS

I T is not very easy for villagers to know the exact time by Greenwich. When the wind is favourable we sometimes hear the distant boom of the Aldershot gun which is discharged at one o'clock in the day and at 9.30 p.m., or the more prosaic sound of the steam-whistle of a neighbouring timber-works. Some village churches can boast of a clock, an old and venerable piece of mechanism which is guaranteed not to keep very accurate time. Moreover, it has only one hand and can only tell the hours, and the minutes have to be conjectured. But we have our sundials, and in the days before cheap watches abounded they were the only means for telling the time.

These were often placed on the south wall of the church or on the tower, and when the sun shone upon it and indicated that the hour of Divine service was approaching, the clerk began to ring one of the bells or the ringers rang a merry peal. When the sun refused to shine, or when the nights were dark and the clerk had to ring the curfew, the time must have been somewhat uncertain unless he possessed a clock.

The sundial often stands in the churchyard upon a

151

pedestal, or when the upper part of the churchyard cross
has perished the stem has been used for the purpose. Chil-
ham churchyard, Kent, has a very beautiful sundial with a
very graceful stone pedestal designed by Inigo Jones. At
Kilham, East Yorkshire, a stone coffin sunk into the ground
has been used as the stem of a sundial which was placed
there in 1769.[1] We give an illustration of the massive sundial which stands in the churchyard of Elmley Castle village,
Worcestershire. Viewed in the framework of the ancient
doorway of the church-porch with the village beyond, it
forms a very pleasing object. These primitive timekeepers
are often adorned with ornamental ironwork, produced by
the skill of the village blacksmith, and bear appropriate inscriptions. There is a very curious one cut in stone near
the sundial at Seaham Church, Durham :

> The natural clockwork by the Mighty One
> Wound up at first, and ever since has gone :
> No pin drops out, its wheels and springs are good,
> It speaks its Maker's praise tho' once it stood ;
> But that was by the order of the Workman's power;
> And when it stands again it goes no more.

There is a very charming inscription on the sundial in
Shenstone churchyard, near Lichfield. It runs :

> If o'er the dial glides a shade, redeem
> The time ; for, lo, it passes like a dream.
> But if 'tis all a blank, then mark the loss
> Of hours unblest by shadows from the cross.

The dial is formed by a cross surmounting a pillar, the cross
being placed in a leaning position, the arms of which cast
shadows on the figures engraved on the sides of the shaft.

Others content themselves with simpler rhymes, sententious
mottoes, or appropriate texts from the Bible, such as the inscription at Isleworth, Middlesex, which runs :

> Watch and pray.
> Time passeth away like a shadow.

[1] *Curious Church Customs*, by W. Andrews, p. 156.

THE SUNDIAL IN ELMLEY CASTLE VILLAGE CHURCHYARD,
WORCESTERSHIRE

THE CHARM OF THE ENGLISH VILLAGE

The motto on an ancient dial at Millrigg, near Penrith, inscribed by some member of the Order of Knights Hospitallers of St. John of Jerusalem, is worth recording. It is in the form of a dialogue between the dial personified and the passenger :

Diall

Staie, Passinger.
Tell me thy name,
        Thy nature.

*Pass*r

Thy name is die
All. I a mort all
    creation.

Diall

Since my name
And thy nature
    Soe agree,
Thinke on thy selfe
When thov looks
    Upon me.

The Eyam sundial is remarkable. It has the names of several places inscribed upon it in order to show the differences of time, and also the tropics are marked with the motto :

Induce animum sapientem, 1773.

The multiplication of clocks and watches has rendered the use of sundials obsolete. But though rare in villages, clocks can claim a considerable antiquity. Peter Lightfoot, a monk of Glastonbury, was an ingenious maker who fashioned in 1335 for his monastery a wonderful clock which not only told the time, but made some figures move so as to represent a knightly tournament. Another of his works of skill exists at Wimborne Minster. Some village clockmakers two hundred years ago were very clever, and have left us some admirable "grandfathers" which are now eagerly sought by collectors. I have been fortunate enough to acquire three such clocks, two of which date from the end of the seventeenth century. Villagers are very skilful in knowing the time without referring either to clock or watch, and their wits are especially keen when the dinner-hour is approaching.

They are also remarkable prophets concerning the weather and the changes in the direction of the wind. They watch the vane on the church spire, and homely rhymes enable them to prophesy what the weather will be. Thus the Wiltshire peasant tells :

> When the wind is north-west
> The weather is at the best ;
> If the rain comes out of the east,
> 'Twill rain twice twenty-four hours at the least.

Another rhyme assures us :

> A southerly wind with showers of rain,
> Will bring the wind from west again.

The north wind brings snow, wet, and cold. A north-east wind is neither good for man nor beast. But

> The wind in the west
> Suits every one best.

The villagers can tell the kind of weather to be expected from watching the animals, who are famous prophets. Thus, an ass's bray foretells rain. The bees stay at home when it is likely to be wet. A crowing cock at even, or a bawling peacock, prognosticates rain. High-flying rooks or low-flying swallows predict bad weather ; and

> When black snails cross your path
> Black clouds much moisture hath.

Whatever may be the value of this weather-wisdom, the vane on the church spire never lies. It is a beautiful and graceful object, which again bears witness to the skill of the village blacksmith. Its form is traditional, and has been handed down to our own day from the time of St. Dunstan. Its popular name weather-*cock* suggests its shape. Why was this bird selected to preside over our spires and turrets ?

It is the emblem of vigilance. Hugo de Sancto Victore, in the *Mystical Mirrour of the Church*, tells us :

" The cock representeth the preacher. For the cock in the deep watches of the night divideth the hours thereof with his song, and arouseth the sleepers. He foretelleth the approach of day, but first he stirreth up himself to crow by the striking of his wings. Behold ye these things mystically, for not one of them is there without meaning. The sleepers be the children of this world lying in sins. The cock is the company of preachers, which do preach sharply, do stir up the sleepers to cast away the works of darkness, which also do foretell the coming of the light, when they preach of the Day of Judgment and of future glory. But wisely before they preach unto others do they rouse themselves by virtue from the sleep of sin and do chasten their bodies."

There was a weathercock on the cathedral of Winchester in 961 A.D., and Wulstan relates how it caught the morning sun and filled the traveller with amazement :

" The golden weathercock lording it over the city ; up there he stands over the heads of the men of Winchester, and up in mid-air seems nobly to rule the western world ; in the claw is the sceptre of command, and like the all-vigilant eye of the ruler, it turns every way."

Constant allusions to the erection of weathercocks are found in old records. Although the cock was the usual symbol, other forms may be found occasionally. A ship is sometimes seen surmounting the steeple, and the symbol of the saint to whom the church is dedicated is occasionally selected as a vane. Thus, in London, St. Peter's, Cornhill, has a key ; St. Lawrence, Jewry, a gridiron ; St. Botolph's, Aldgate, an arrow ; and St. Clement Danes, an anchor.

But weathercocks are not confined to churches, and our artist has discovered several excellent examples of domestic vanes that grace the roofs of farm buildings, half-timbered houses, and humbler dwellings. In former days it was considered an important privilege to be allowed to set up a vane, and no one was permitted to erect a weathercock upon his house unless he were descended from a noble family. Indeed, some ancient authors assert that none could attain to that honour who had not been foremost at scaling the walls in an assault upon some city, or had first planted their banners on the ramparts. The form of these domestic vanes was usually the armorial bearings of the family, the crest or banner. The arrow, cock, and banner are common designs. Thus, at Clun, Salop, there is an arrow, and at Leominster a half-timbered house called the Grange has a banner inscribed with the date 1687.

CLUN, SALOP

It is interesting to note that this house was formerly the old town hall built by John Abel (see p. 118), and that when the townspeople wanted to demolish the structure it was bought by Mr. Arkwright and re-erected in his grounds as a residence. The beautiful ironwork of this example should be noticed. The dovecote at Eardisland has a fish for its vane, and a cock and a hound are other forms shown in the illustrations. Even the cottage at Mansell Lacy, Herefordshire, has a little vane. It is a curious Herefordshire custom, notes our artist, to place a twig at the finish of the thatch in such a manner that it will revolve. To this twig is affixed the figure of a bird made out of thatching-straw, the whole thus serving the purpose of a weathercock. The accuracy of such a vane, I should imagine,

HALF-TIMBER HOUSE, CALLED THE GRANGE, LEOMINSTER

may be a questionable matter, but that it revolves somewhat there is no doubt. It forms a very pleasing finish to
the ridge of a thatched roof.

We have not exhausted the charms of our village. That
would be a large volume which recorded all its attractions.

There is the fascination of the wild-life,
the birds and beasts, the butterflies and
insects, that dwell in the neighbouring
woodland, the treasures of the trout-
stream with its medley of exquisite
things, where many a tiny creature finds
sanctuary, undisturbed by the world's
rude noise or the tread of the tourist.
That wood is a haven of rest, a temple
of silence broken only by the song of
the birds, the sudden cry of a jay, or the
scamper of a rabbit in the undergrowth.
The beauty of the wild flowers—honey-
suckles, mints, St. John's wort, wild roses,
wild thyme, and a host of others—constitute a charm that never fails to please,
for those who love Nature's treasures.
The colours change in the glowing carpet

THE DOVECOTE,
EARDISLAND,
HEREFORDSHIRE

of the woods. Now it is yellow with
primroses ; now blue with wild hyacinths ; now the giant bracken puts forth

its head shaped like a shepherd's crook, and soon it grows
as high as one's head ; and as the autumn season advances
it turns its green fronds into dull gold that glisten in the
sunlight. Even in winter the woods lose not their beauty
and their charm.

And now I come to the greatest charm of all, far greater
than storied minster, palatial manor, or picturesque cottage,
and that is the villagers themselves. Perhaps some day
I may tell you more about them. They are the real charm

of our picture. All that I have told you is the framework. I could tell you strange stories of their beliefs, their superstitions, their shrewdness, their old-fashioned courtesies, their gentlemanliness, their sturdiness and bravery. But that is another story, and must be left for a future time.

We have tried to paint the picture of our village, and to see all its graces and perfections. Mr. Sydney R. Jones,

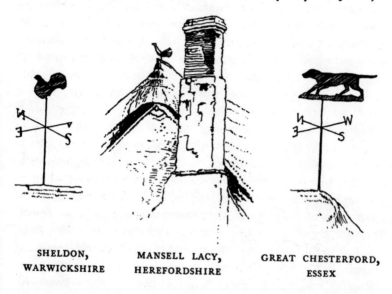

| SHELDON, WARWICKSHIRE | MANSELL LACY, HEREFORDSHIRE | GREAT CHESTERFORD, ESSEX |

has drawn them with skilful pen, and I have but endeavoured to point out their many beauties. I have told little of the buried treasures that this hamlet holds, little of the lore and legend, little of the great men who have lived here and added honour to our annals. The parish chest is still locked, and the documents at the record office I have severely left alone. But we have seen how our village grew up from babyhood to man's estate—I will not allow that even now it is very old, or getting into its dotage—we have looked upon its treasures, its wealth of beauty, its rural homesteads, its paradise of flowers. We have admired the wondrous skill of our forefathers who wrought so surely and so well, and so effectively used the materials which Nature gave them, whether stone or brick or timber, tile or slate, and thus discovered the true secret of the harmony with nature, the chief characteristic of English village architecture. We may learn something from their example. We may learn to abstain from spoiling their work by the erection of cheap and inferior buildings which degrade the landscape by their crude colours and graceless form. We may learn to adhere to the same principles which guided them, cultivate the same means, and imbue our minds with the same sense of harmony and reverence for antiquity, and then the charm of the English village will not be allowed to decay. Can it not be retained? Cottages that are insanitary can be improved and made sanitary without being pulled down. Small holdings may attract new-comers, and honest, thrifty labourers may become their own masters and farm their own land. We who live in the country are a little incredulous about the results of the laws which some of those good members of Parliament who know nothing about us frame for our benefit; but if in their wisdom they can devise anything to improve our conditions of life, we shall not be ungrateful. Sometimes we, whose lot it is to live in an English village, sigh for a larger outlook, a more extended sphere of work, for contact with kindred souls in the great world of art, literature, or science; but life in the country is wondrously attractive to those who love nature, and we are thankful that we have been called to work amidst the fields and lanes of rural England, and are able to appreciate the charm of an English village.

FINIS

INDEX

INDEX

Epitaphs, 24

Essex, external plaster (pargetting) from, 73

Evelyn's description of the squire's garden, 83

Evolution of the modern mansion, 44-5

Ewelme, Oxon., 111, 112, 117

Eyam, cross at, 121; sundial at, 154

F

Farleigh Hungerford, Somerset, 5, 8

Farmhouses, 42

" Filling in " of half-timber work, 57

Flowers in cottage gardens, 86, 90-2; names of, 90

Flyford Flavel, Worcestershire, interior of the Union Inn, 97, 99

Fonts, 28

Footbridges, 150

Fordwich, Kent, the Town-hall, 131, 132

Foreign villages compared with English, 1

Formal gardens, 92

Fulling mill at East Hendred, 104

G

Galleting or garneting, 62

Garden of cottage, 49, 84-94

Garden paths, 88

Gardens, village, 83-94

Garnacott (near Bideford). A cottage fire-place, 74, 78

Garway, Herefordshire, dovecote at, 139

Geology in its relation to building, 4

Gibbet-irons, 133

Gloves made in Worcestershire, 106

"God's Acre," 23

God's hostels, 111-14

Godshill village, Isle of Wight, 17, 19

Gothic spirit retained, 74, 80

Grammar schools, 116-18

Great Chesterford, Essex, 55, 60; vane at, 159

Great Coxwell, 134, 137

Great Tew, Oxon., cottages at, 66, 69-71

Greens, village, 20-21, 128-9; crosses on, 125

Guilds for supporting bridges, 146

H

Half-timbered houses, 50-60

Hall, the central, tradition or, 42; diminution in use of, 45

Hants and Dorset, varieties of walling from, 57

Harvington, Worcestershire. The Haunted Hall, 37, 38

Haunted houses, 38

Heraldic arms on houses, 51, 74; as weathercocks, 157

Herefordshire: cottage vanes, 157-8; market-houses, 118; John Abel's work in, 118

Herring-bone work, 58

Herts, external plaster details (pargetting), from, 73

Hexham, cross at, 121

Highwaymen, 133

Highworth, barn at, 136

Hinxton, Cambridgeshire, 62, 65

Horsham stone, 63-4

Hour-glass in pulpits, 30, 32

Hurley, Berks, pigeon-house at, 138

Hurstmonceux Castle, Sussex, 35, 36-7

I

Ilkley, cross at, 121

INDEX

INDEX

Villages, English, beauty of, 1, 2, 22 ; characteristics of, 17–22 ; compared with foreign, 1 ; industries of, 102–110 ; stability of, 2 ; variety of, 2, 3

W

Walling, great variety of, 57, 62
Wantage, almshouse at, 111
Wargrave, inn at, 100
Watermills, village, 106, 107, 108
Watlington, Oxon. The market-house, 13
Wayside crosses, 125
Weathercocks, 155–8
Weather-lore, 155
Weobley, Herefordshire, 3, 8 ; porch of the old grammar school, 117, 118
West Hendred, Berks, a garden at, 93–4

West Wycombe, Bucks, 13, 14
Whalley, crosses, 119
Whipping-posts, 130
Whittington, sundial at, 151
Wild flowers, 158
Wild-life of the country, 158
Winchcombe, coat-of-arms from, 74
Winchester, vane at, 156
Windows, cottage, 79, 82
Window-gardens, 88–9
Windmills, 108
Winson, Gloucestershire, cottages at, 48, 50
Woodmen, 108
Wool, Dorset. The manor-house and bridge, 40, 41
Worksworth quarries, 6

Y

Yeoman's house, the, 42